DEDICATION

To my lifelong friend Dave.
You have been a huge part of my life and
I wouldn't trade the memories we have for anything.

CONTENTS

ACKNOWLEDGMENTS

I want to thank everyone who has attended my classes,
welcomed me into their homes & businesses,
attended my cooking shows, bought my books, travelled with me,
and has been a dedicated reader of my columns.

Without you… none of this would be a reality.
Thank you all so much.

SPREADS, DIPS, & SALSAS

Artichoke and Asiago Dip

Blueberry Salsa

Chipotle Mayonnaise

Fresh Cut Salsa

Fresh Guacamole

Pineapple Salsa

Spinach and Artichoke Dip

Strawberry Salsa

Tzatziki

Artichoke & Asiago Dip

1 cup mayonnaise
1/2 cup drained minced canned artichokes
50g grated Asiago cheese, approx. 1/2 cup
1/2 to 1 garlic clove, finely crushed or minced
1 tsp lemon juice
1/2 tsp salt
1/2 tsp liquid honey
1/2 tsp sweet smoked paprika, optional

1. Mix everything together and serve with crackers or tortilla chips.

Makes approximately 2 cups

Blueberry Salsa

"The contrast of the fresh blueberries with the other ingredients is absolutely mouthwatering"

1 medium yellow bell pepper diced small
1/2 jalapeno, minced – seeds & membrane removed for a milder salsa
1/4 cup small diced red onion
2 – 4 tbsp finely chopped fresh mint
Zest from 1 lime, finely chopped
2 tbsp lime juice
1 tsp sugar
1 tsp fresh cracked black pepper
1/4 tsp salt
1.5 (one and one half) cups fresh blueberries

1. Mix all of the ingredients together, except for the blueberries.
2. Gently toss in the fresh blueberries into the salsa ingredients.
3. Serve the salsa over the grilled chicken or fish.

Makes approximately 2 cups

Chipotle Mayonnaise

"Canned chipotle peppers from the Mexican foods section of your grocery store are an easy way to spice up mayonnaise for an incredible dipping sauce or sandwich spread"

1 cup mayonnaise
1 or 2 canned chipotle peppers

1. Add the ingredients to a food processor – start with 1 chipotle pepper.
2. Puree until smooth. Taste and add an additional pepper if you want it spicier (then process again).
3. Serve immediately as a dipping sauce or sandwich spread, or keep chilled in the refrigerator.

Makes just over 1 cup

Fresh Cut Salsa

"By rinsing and draining the diced red onion, the onion flavour won't be overpowering, but will still provide nice colour. Omit the seeds and white membrane from the jalapeno for a milder salsa."

3 large Roma tomatoes, diced small
1 small yellow bell pepper, diced small
1/2 long English cucumber, diced small
1 cup small diced red onion, rinsed and drained
1 jalapeno, diced very small
1 – 2 garlic cloves, finely crushed or minced
Juice of 1 lime
1 tsp sugar
Salt & Pepper to taste
Fresh chopped cilantro, to taste

1. Mix everything together and serve immediately.

Makes approximately 4 cups

Fresh Guacamole

2 soft avocados
Juice from 1 large lime
1/4 yellow bell pepper, finely diced
1/4 red bell pepper, finely diced
1/4 red onion, finely diced
1/2 jalapeno pepper, minced
1 garlic clove, finely crushed or minced
1/2 tsp ground cumin
1/2 tsp sambal oelek
1/2 tsp sugar
salt & pepper, to taste

1. Cut, pit, and peel the avocados. Mash them in a medium bowl with the lime juice.
2. Add all of the other ingredients to the bowl and mix together. Refrigerate until needed.

Pineapple Salsa

Diced fresh Pineapple, approximately 1.5 (one and one half) cups
1 medium red bell pepper diced small
1/2 jalapeno, minced – seeds & membrane removed for a milder salsa
1/4 cup small diced red onion
2 – 4 tbsp finely chopped fresh mint
Zest from 1 lime, finely chopped
2 tbsp lime juice
1.5 (one and one half) tsp sugar
1 tsp fresh cracked black pepper
1/4 tsp salt

1. Mix all ingredients together.

Makes approximately 2 cups

Spinach Artichoke Dip

"Served with tortilla chips, this will be one of the best appetizers at any party"

250g package cream cheese, room temperature
1.5 (one and one half) cups sour cream
1 cup mayonnaise
100g – 150g mozzarella cheese, grated
2 cans artichoke hearts, drained and chopped
2 – 300g packages frozen chopped spinach, thawed and drained
2 garlic cloves, crushed
2 - 3 tbsp red wine vinegar
1/2 tsp sambal oelek
Salt & fresh cracked pepper to taste

1. Preheat oven to 350 degrees.
2. Thoroughly combine the sour cream into the cream cheese.
3. Stir in the mayonnaise, mozzarella, artichokes, spinach, garlic, red wine vinegar, and sambal oelek.
4. Season to taste with salt and pepper.
5. Transfer to an oven-proof dish and bake for approximately 50 to 60 minutes until completely heated through. Serve immediately with tortilla chips for dipping.

Makes approximately 6 cups

Strawberry Salsa

10 strawberries, diced small, approximately 1.5 cups
1 medium yellow bell pepper diced small
1/2 jalapeno, minced – seeds & membrane removed for a milder salsa
1/4 cup small diced red onion
2 – 4 tbsp finely chopped fresh mint
zest from 1 lime, finely chopped
2 tbsp lime juice
1.5 tsp sugar
1 tsp fresh cracked black pepper
1/4 tsp salt

1. Mix all ingredients together.
2. Serve over grilled chicken or fish.

Makes approximately 2 cups

Greek Tzatziki

1 long English cucumber, grated
500g plain yogurt
3-4 garlic cloves, crushed
1 tbsp finely chopped fresh dill
1 tbsp olive oil
salt and pepper to season

1. Put grated cucumbers in a clean towel or cheesecloth and squeeze to remove moisture.
2. Place drained cucumbers in a bowl, and add all the other ingredients; stir to combine.

Makes approximately 3 cups

APPETIZERS

Broiled Greek Tomatoes

Cheddar Sesame Crackers

Creamy Stuffed Mushrooms

Honey Garlic Hot Wings

Loaded Nachos

Honey Garlic Meatballs

Sweet & Sour Meatballs

Pan Seared Sage Scallops

Salt & Pepper Pita Chips

Rosemary Maple Bacon Jam

Spanikopita

Broiled Greek Tomatoes

12 medium Roma tomatoes, room temperature
Salt & freshly cracked pepper
1/3 cup finely chopped fresh oregano
Extra virgin olive oil
150g-200g crumbled feta cheese

1. Slice the tomatoes lengthwise (from top to bottom) into halves. Place the 24 halves, cut side up on a baking sheet (line with parchment for easy clean up). *Tip – slice a thin piece off the skin side (the side that will be on the baking sheet) to help them sit more steady.
2. Season liberally with salt and fresh cracked pepper.
3. Distribute the amount of chopped oregano evenly on the tomatoes.
4. Drizzle a small amount of olive oil on each tomato.
5. Distribute the feta cheese evenly on the tomatoes. *Tip – hold each tomato half over the cheese bowl to catch any cheese that falls off, and then return them to the baking sheet.
6. Broil under a hot preheated broiler for approximately 4 to 5 minutes until the cheese is slightly browned.

Makes 24 halves

Cheddar Sesame Crackers

Recipe created by Katherine Desormeaux (Mrs. Chef Dez)

2 cups whole wheat flour
2 cups grated old cheddar cheese
3 tablespoons sugar
1 teaspoon salt
1/4 tsp paprika
1/4 tsp ground cayenne (optional)
1/2 cup butter, frozen
1/2 cup water
Extra whole wheat flour for rolling
1/2 cup sesame seeds

1. Preheat your oven to 450 degrees Fahrenheit.
2. Mix the flour, cheddar, sugar, salt, paprika, cayenne together in a bowl. Using a standard cheese grater, grate the frozen butter into this dry mixture and toss to mix. Add the water and mix until just combined to form a dough. Cut the dough into four equal parts.
3. Flatten out one portion of dough in your hands and sprinkle a small amount of flour on the counter and on top of the portion of the dough. Start rolling out the dough while ensuring the underside stays well floured. When the top of the dough starts to stick to the rolling pin sprinkle it with a generous amount of sesame seeds and roll the seeds onto the dough until it is approximately 1/8th of an inch thick. Note: if you use too much flour on the top of the dough, the sesame seeds will not stick; the seeds will help to keep the dough from sticking to the rolling pin. Cut the rolled dough into desired shapes and place on an ungreased baking sheet. Bake for approximately 5 to 6 minutes or until they have just turned brown. Because of the cheddar cheese and sesame seeds they must be watched closely to ensure they don't burn. Remove from the baking sheet to cool on a wire rack. Repeat with the other 3 portions of dough.
4. When completely cooled, store in an air-tight container at room temperature for up to 5 days. Makes 4 to 5 dozen crackers.

Creamy Stuffed Mushrooms

24 large white button mushrooms
1 tbsp oil
1 tbsp butter
4 garlic cloves, minced
1 small onion, finely chopped
1 tsp salt
1/2 tsp fresh cracked pepper
1 cup cream cheese, room temperature
1/4 cup grated parmesan cheese
1 – 170g can crabmeat, drained
1/2 cup grated Mozzarella cheese

1. Preheat oven to 400 degrees.
2. Remove the stems from the mushrooms and chop finely, leaving the mushroom caps intact and set aside in a baking dish.
3. Add the oil and butter to a large nonstick pan over medium heat. Once the butter has melted, add the chopped mushroom stems, garlic, onion, salt and pepper. Cook until all vegetables are soft and the liquid has evaporated, approximately 7 to 10 minutes, stirring occasionally.
4. Stir in the cream cheese and the parmesan cheese. Once fully combined remove from the heat and stir in the crabmeat. Season to taste.
5. Fill the mushroom caps equally with the stuffing and place back in the baking dish. Bake for approximately 20 to 25 minutes until tender. Place under the broiler until golden brown if needed. Let cool slightly before serving.

Makes 24 stuffed mushrooms

Honey Garlic Hot Wings

"The best of both worlds – Honey Garlic Wings and Hot Wings all in one. Make sure you serve these with napkins!"

1 cup liquid honey
1 head of garlic (8 to 10 cloves), finely crushed or minced
3 to 4 tbsp sambal oelek
1 tbsp chili powder
1 tsp cinnamon
Zest from 2 limes, chopped fine
Juice from 2 limes
Dash of ground cloves
Dash of ground nutmeg
Salt & pepper
2 kg chicken wings
1 to 2 tbsp cornstarch

1. Mix all of the ingredients together (except for the wings and the cornstarch) in a bowl. Put the chicken wings in a large freezer bag and pour this mixture onto the wings. Seal the bag and distribute this marinade around the wings thoroughly. Let sit in the refrigerator for at least 2 to 4 hours.
2. Preheat the oven to 400 degrees.
3. Lay the wings in a single layer on a large baking sheet. Pour the remaining marinade into a pot.
4. Bake the wings for approximately 25 to 30 minutes until cooked through. While the wings are baking, bring the marinade to a boil over medium-high heat and let boil for approximately one minute, stirring constantly.
5. After the wings have baked, drain the excess liquid from the baking sheet into the marinade in the pot, while keeping the wings on the baking sheet.
6. Mix the cornstarch with a few tablespoons of water until completely dissolved. Stir this cornstarch mixture into the hot marinade. Bring this back to a boil, stirring constantly, and it should transform into a thick sauce almost resembling a paste.
7. Distribute this thickened sauce onto the wings evenly. Return the wings to the oven and broil until the sauce has browned slightly, and caramelized onto the wings.
8. Remove from the oven and let cool slightly before serving.

Loaded Nachos

"This will be the biggest display of nachos you have seen! Seasoning each layer with salt, pepper, and chili powder helps to make these very flavourful.

1 to 1.5 pounds lean ground beef
1 package taco seasoning
1 bunch green onions, sliced
375ml can sliced black olives, drained
3 medium tomatoes, diced small, drained
2 – 3 jalapenos, sliced into rings
600g old cheddar, grated
1.5 - 340g bags thick nacho chips
Salt & pepper
Chili powder
Salsa & sour cream, for serving

1. Brown the ground beef with the taco seasoning and set aside.
2. On a 12 x 18 baking sheet make 3 layers with all the ingredients divided equally. Build each layer in the following order:

Nacho Chips
Cheese
Seasoned Beef
Tomatoes
Black Olives
Green Onions
Jalapenos
Salt & Pepper
Chili Powder
More Cheese

3. The baking sheet will be full and heaped with ingredients. Bake in a pre-heated 350-degree oven for 10 to 15 minutes until cheese has melted and the nachos are completely warmed through.
4. Serve immediately with side dishes of salsa and sour cream.

Serves 4 to 8 people.

Honey Garlic Meatballs

"Combining two different types of meat gives the meatballs more complex flavour and seasoned with Chinese 5 Spice powder they are perfect with this sauce. Ground chuck is beef but has more flavour than ground beef from the supermarket – visit your local butcher to get some."

1 pound (454g) ground chuck
1 pound (454g) lean ground pork
2 large eggs
1/2 cup fine bread crumbs
1/4 cup minced onion
2 tbsp finely crushed or minced garlic
1 tbsp Chinese 5 Spice powder
2 tsp salt
1 tsp pepper

Sauce
1 cup + 2 tbsp beef broth
3/4 cup dark brown sugar
1/2 cup liquid honey
6 tbsp soy sauce
3 tbsp cornstarch
1.5 tbsp finely crushed garlic
1/2 tsp salt

1. Preheat oven to 400 degrees Fahrenheit. Spray a baking sheet with baking spray and set aside.
2. In a large bowl, combine the chuck, pork, eggs, bread crumbs, onion, garlic, 5 spice, 2 tsp salt & the pepper. Mix until thoroughly combined into a homogenous mixture. Roll bits of the mixture into small meatballs approximately 3/4-inch in size and place them on the prepared baking sheet. You should have approximately 45 to 50 meatballs. Bake in the preheated oven for approximately 20 minutes, or until their internal temperature reaches 160 degrees Fahrenheit (71 degrees Celsius).

3. While the meatballs are cooking, prepare the sauce by placing the beef broth, brown sugar, honey, soy sauce, cornstarch, garlic and half tsp salt in a medium heavy-bottomed pot. Place on medium-high heat and bring to a boil stirring occasionally. When it just starts to boil stir constantly until it has reached a full rolling boil. It must reach a full boil to activate the cornstarch thickener fully. Remove from the heat and set aside.
4. Place the cooked meatballs on paper towel temporarily to remove some of the fat. Transfer the meatballs to a serving dish, cover with the sauce and serve immediately with or without cooked rice.

Makes 45 to 50, 3/4 inch meatballs

Sweet & Sour Meatballs

Use the same recipe & instructions from the Honey Garlic Meatballs, except substitute 1 tablespoon chilli powder for the 1 tablespoon Chinese 5 spice powder, and use these sauce ingredients instead for the sauce:

Sauce
2 cups white sugar
1 & 1/2 cups white vinegar
1/2 cup brown sugar
1/2 cup ketchup
1/2 cup soy sauce
4 & 1/2 tbsp cornstarch

Pan Seared Sage Scallops

12 large scallops
Salt & Pepper
1 – 2 tsp grape-seed oil or canola oil
1/3 cup cold butter, cubed into tbsp pieces
2 tbsp chopped fresh sage

1. Preheat a heavy bottomed medium/large pan over medium-high heat until it is very hot.
2. Pat dry the scallops and season them on both sides with salt & pepper.
3. Add the oil to the pan and then immediately add the scallops one or two at a time. Cook in the hot pan for about 30 seconds to a minute on the one side until they are seared/browned.
4. Flip them over, cook for another 30 seconds, then add the butter pieces one or two at a time until it has all been added. The butter will brown very quickly and immediately add the sage, stir and coat the scallops with the infused brown butter sauce and serve immediately.

Salt & Pepper Pita Chips

6 "pocket style" pita breads
Olive oil, salt, and fresh cracked pepper

1. Preheat oven to 450 degrees.
2. With a sharp knife, separate the top and bottom halves from each pita pocket to create 2 rounds from each bread.
3. Brush both sides of the rounds with olive oil.
4. Cut each round in half and then each half into 4 equal pie shaped chips. Place these chips on a baking sheet and dust with salt and fresh cracked pepper.
5. Bake for approximately 4 to 6 minutes until mostly golden brown. You may want to rotate the pans half way through the baking time.

Makes 96 chips

Rosemary Maple Bacon Jam

"The perfect topping for almost any appetizers you may be thinking of offering to your guests, like bruscetta, cheese & crackers, canapés, etc. My favorite is paired with soft unripened goat cheese (chevre) as the creamy tanginess is the perfect match for this sweet complex concoction."

1 pound bacon slices, cut into 1/4 inch pieces
2 medium onions, quartered and sliced thin
6 to 8 garlic cloves, chopped
1 cup black coffee
2/3 cup packed brown sugar
1/2 cup maple syrup
1/3 cup apple cider vinegar
1 tbsp finely chopped fresh rosemary

1. Add the bacon pieces to a large heavy bottomed pan or dutch oven. Turn the heat to medium/high and cook the bacon until almost crisp (browned and cooked, but not crisp), reducing the heat to medium as it starts to turn brown, stirring occasionally, approximately 20 minutes. Remove the cooked bacon with a slotted spoon and set aside on paper towels to drain.
2. Remove all but 1 tablespoon of the bacon fat from the pan. Turn the heat to medium and stir in the onions to the tablespoon of bacon fat followed by the garlic. Cook, stirring occasionally, until this onion/garlic mixture is softened and slightly browned, approximately 5 to 7 minutes.
3. Add the coffee, brown sugar, maple syrup, vinegar, rosemary, and reserved bacon. Stir to combine and increase the heat to medium/high to bring to a boil. Once boiling, reduce the heat to medium/low and simmer uncovered for approximately 90 minutes until the mixture is syrupy and has a jam like texture.
4. Transfer this mixture to a food processor and pulse a few times until the consistency/texture is what you desire. Will last up to 3 weeks in your refrigerator.

Makes approximately 2 cups

Spanikopita

"Little triangular pastry pockets of spinach & feta cheese. A Greek favourite."

2 tbsp butter
1/4 cup minced onion
2 garlic cloves, minced
1 – 300g package frozen chopped spinach, thawed & drained well
100g feta cheese, crumbled
1 tbsp fresh lemon juice
Salt & pepper to taste
10 sheets frozen phyllo pastry, thawed, covered with parchment & damp towel
Melted butter

1. Melt butter over medium heat in a nonstick pan.
2. Add the onions and garlic and sauté until soft, about 2 minutes.
3. Add the spinach and cook stirring until all the moisture has evaporated.
4. Transfer this mixture to a bowl and let cool.
5. Preheat the oven to 375 degrees.
6. Stir in the Feta cheese, lemon juice, salt & pepper and set aside.
7. Take one sheet of pastry and place horizontally on the counter; brush half with melted butter (right or left side) and then fold the unbuttered half over the buttered half
8. Cut lengthwise into four strips.
9. Place approximately 1 teaspoon of filling on the bottom left corner of each strip. Fold over the right side to meet the left to form a triangle. Continue folding in this manner until you have reached the top, and tuck in any loose ends at the end of folding.
10. Place on a parchment covered baking sheet. Brush each triangle with more melted butter.
11. Bake for approximately 15 minutes, until golden brown and serve warm.

Yield: 40 pieces.

*Tip – these can be made in advance and frozen before baking. To freeze them individually place the baking sheet in the freezer after step 10 until frozen, then gently transfer them to a container with a tightly sealed lid and place back in the freezer. Keep frozen for up to 3 months. Bake from frozen on parchment covered baking sheet for 20 minutes.

SALADS

Corn, Date & Goat Cheese Salads

Blueberry Cobb Salad

Caesar Salad Dressing

Fat Free Coleslaw Dressing

Greek Salad

Greek Tabbouleh Salad

Grilled Potato Salad

Grilled Vegetable Salad with Blueberry Vinaigrette

Mediterranean Salad Dressing

Mushroom Salad with Spicy Bacon Dressing

Pumpkin Vinaigrette

South-Western Steak Salads

Quick & Easy Oil & Vinegar Salad Dressing

Warm Bacon Dressing

Corn, Date, and Goat Cheese Salads

"Contrasting flavours at their finest. Loose baking dates in a bag are easier to prepare than from a brick of dates or fresh dates."

3 cups corn kernels
1 red bell pepper, diced small
1 & 1/3 packed cups of loose baking dates, finely chopped
2 large jalapeno peppers, diced small, seeds and inner membrane removed
1/2 cup finely chopped red onion
2 garlic cloves, crushed
1/4 cup extra virgin olive oil
1/4 cup balsamic vinegar
Salt & pepper to taste
Enough mixed greens for 6-8 people
200g soft unripened goat cheese

1. Mix together the corn, bell pepper, dates, jalapenos, red onion, garlic, olive oil, balsamic, salt & pepper.
2. Make individual mounds of greens for each person.
3. Top equally with the corn mixture from step one, and then the crumbled goat cheese.

Makes 6 to 8 portions

Blueberry Cobb Salad

"To celebrate British Columbia's 150th Birthday, I wrote this version of cob salad with ingredients that are the same colours as our BC flag – Blue, Red, Yellow, and White."

5 strips of bacon, cut into small pieces
1 clove of garlic
1/4 cup red wine vinegar
1 tbsp lemon juice
1 tbsp sugar
1 tsp Worcestershire sauce
1 tsp salt
1/2 tsp pepper
1/4 tsp dry ground mustard
1/2 cup extra virgin olive oil

1. Cook the bacon in a frying pan until crisp. Reserve the rendered fat.
2. Place the bacon and the garlic in a food processor and process until minced.
3. Add the reserved bacon fat to the food processor along with all of the remaining ingredients, except for the extra virgin olive oil. Puree on high speed.
4. With the food processor still on high speed, slowly add the olive oil until thoroughly combined. Makes approximately 1 cup of dressing.

2 large romaine hearts
2 cups (1 pint) fresh blueberries
3 hard boiled eggs, peeled, quartered, and cut into small chunks
1 cup quartered cherry tomatoes
1 cup crumbled mild blue cheese ~or~ 1 cup crumbled feta cheese
1 cup drained canned corn kernels
1 red bell pepper, cut into thin 1-inch strips, approx. 1 cup

1. Cut the romaine hearts into small bite size pieces. Wash thoroughly and spin dry in a salad spinner. If the romaine is too wet it will water-down the taste of the dressing. Place on a large deep serving platter

that will be big enough for tossing before serving. The romaine should be placed evenly across the platter (not mounded up).

2. By the time you have finished assembling the salad, you should have seven equal strips of ingredients covering the romaine lettuce. Start with first putting two strips of blueberries (1 cup for each strip) on each end of the pile of lettuce.

3. Then working left to right (from one strip of blueberries to the other) place the remaining ingredients in equal sized strips on the romaine lettuce: eggs, tomatoes, blue cheese, corn, and red pepper. You are now finished assembling the salad and the romaine lettuce should be completely covered with seven strips of ingredients that are the same colour as the BC Flag. Bring to the table to display with the vinaigrette separate.

4. Just before serving, pour the dressing over the salad and toss thoroughly.

Makes approximately 4 portions as a meal, or 6 to 8 as a side dish

Caesar Salad Dressing

"Do not substitute whole egg for the egg yolks – egg yolks are an emulsifier that will keep this dressing from separating"

1 tbsp fresh lemon juice
1 tbsp white wine vinegar
1 tbsp Dijon mustard
1 tsp Worcestershire sauce
2 dashes tobasco sauce
3 canned anchovies
3 crushed garlic cloves
2 egg yolks
2 tbsp dry dill
1/2 tsp salt
1 cup canola oil

1. Process all of the ingredients, except for the canola oil, in a food processor.
2. With the food processor running at top speed, gradually and the oil in a very slow steady stream until fully incorporated.

Makes approximately 2 cups

Photo credit: Dale Klippenstein

Fat Free Coleslaw Dressing

"Creamy and flavourful – no one will ever guess that it is fat free"

1 cup no-fat yogurt
1 cup no-fat sour cream
1/4 cup powdered buttermilk
1/4 cup liquid honey
1 tbsp yellow mustard
1 tbsp apple cider vinegar
1 tbsp finely grated red onion
1 tsp Worcestershire sauce
1 tsp salt
1/2 tsp seasoning salt
1/2 tsp freshly ground pepper
1/2 tsp sambal oelek, optional

1. Place all ingredients in a mixing bowl. Whisk thoroughly to combine.
2. Keep refrigerated until needed. Toss with your favorite coleslaw ingredients, like green cabbage, purple cabbage, grated carrots, etc.

Makes approximately 2.5 cups

Greek Salad

2 long English cucumbers, diced large
4 medium tomatoes, or 6-8 Roma tomatoes, diced large
1 large yellow pepper, diced large
1 large orange pepper, diced large
1 medium to large red onion, diced large
1 cup whole kalamata olives

Dressing
1 cup olive oil
1/4 cup fresh lemon juice
3 tbsp red wine vinegar
2 tbsp dried oregano leaves
2 garlic cloves, crushed
2 tbsp sugar
salt and coarsely ground pepper to season

Crumbled feta cheese to garnish

1. In a large bowl, toss the vegetables and olives together.
2. In a separate bowl, mix the dressing ingredients well and pour over the salad. Toss to coat and season to taste with salt and pepper.
3. Garnish with crumbled feta cheese.

Makes approximately 8 to 12 servings

Greek Tabbouleh Salad

"My Greek version of this traditionally Middle Eastern bulgur wheat based salad"

2 cups bulgur wheat
5 cups water
2 tsp salt
3 large garlic cloves, chopped

1. Place the bulgur in a bowl large enough to accommodate all the ingredients above. Combine the water, salt, and garlic in a small pot and bring to a boil.
2. Pour the boiling water mixture over the bulgur, cover and let sit for 30 minutes.
3. Drain the bulgur through a wire mesh sieve and place the drained bulgur/garlic in a large bowl.
4. Add the following ingredients, stir thoroughly to combine and serve immediately or refrigerate to serve later.

2 long English cucumbers, diced small
4 large Roma tomatoes, diced small
1 small yellow bell pepper, diced small
1 medium red onion, diced small
2 cups whole kalamata olives
1/2 cup oil packed sundried tomatoes, drained and diced small
1/4 cup drained capers
250g feta cheese, crumbled
1 tbsp dried oregano leaves
1 tbsp dried basil leaves
1/2 cup extra virgin olive oil
1/4 cup balsamic vinegar
1/4 cup fresh lemon juice
2 tbsp sugar
Salt & pepper to taste

Makes approximately 16 cups of salad

Grilled Potato Salad

"Take a step outside of the ordinary potato salad with this grilled version"

Dressing
1 cup mayonnaise
1 cup sour cream
1/4 cup liquid honey
3 tbsp apple cider vinegar
1 tbsp dried dill
2 tsp Dijon mustard
1 tsp seasoning salt
1/2 tsp fresh ground black pepper
1/2 tsp celery salt
1/4 tsp sambal oelek

Salad Ingredients
1.5kg nugget potatoes
2 large red bell peppers
3 tbsp olive oil
1 bunch green onions
1 large red onion, sliced into thick slices
Salt & Pepper

1. Mix dressing ingredients thoroughly together and refrigerate.
2. Preheat BBQ over high heat.
3. Cut peppers into large pieces and toss with 1 tablespoon of the olive oil. Grill over high heat until charred on both sides and then place in a sealed bowl or paper bag – this will create a steaming environment that will help to loosen the skins on the pepper pieces.
4. Toss the green onions in the residual oil from doing the red peppers and grill over high heat until slightly charred. Remove from grill and set aside.
5. Toss the red onion slices in 1 tablespoon of the olive oil and grill over high heat until caramelized on both sides. Remove from grill and set aside.

6. Toss the potatoes with the remaining 1 tablespoon of olive oil and season with salt & pepper. Grill the potatoes whole over medium to medium-low heat until browned on all sides and cooked through, approximately 12 to 20 minutes (depending on their size). Remove from grill and set aside.
7. Peel the loosened skins from the bell peppers and discard the removed skins
8. Cut the peppers, green onions, and red onions into small pieces.
9. Cut the smallest potatoes in half, and the larger ones into quarters to make consistent bite-sized pieces.
10. Gently toss all of the cut salad ingredients with the dressing and serve immediately. If serving it later, it is important to chill the salad ingredients first before mixing with the dressing to ensure the complete salad stays chilled and keep it out of the bacteria danger zone. Remember to always follow the rule: keep cold foods cold, and keep hot foods hot.

Makes approximately 8 side dish portions

Grilled Vegetable Salad with Blueberry Vinaigrette

"Complex flavour is created by charring vegetables on the BBQ and the blueberries add a complimenting balance of sweetness to the dressing"

<u>Vinaigrette</u>
1.5 (one and one half) cups blueberries
1/4 cup balsamic vinegar
1 garlic clove
1 tbsp lemon juice
1 tsp salt
1/2 tsp pepper
1/2 cup extra virgin olive oil

1. Place all the ingredients, except for the olive oil, in a food processor. Puree on high speed until thoroughly combined.
2. Add the olive oil slowly while the processor is still running. Makes approximately one and a half cups of dressing.

<u>Grilled Vegetable Salad</u>
1 large romaine heart
3 ears of corn, peeled
3 small-medium green zucchinis, sliced thin lengthwise
2 large red bell peppers, quartered, seeds removed
1 large red onion, sliced thick
3 to 4 tbsp olive oil
Salt & pepper
2 to 3 tbsp sunflower seeds

1. Cut the romaine heart into small bite size pieces. Wash thoroughly and spin dry in a salad spinner. If the romaine is too wet it will water-down the taste of the dressing. Place in a large deep bowl that will be big enough for tossing with all of the grilled vegetables.
2. Preheat your grill over high heat.
3. Toss the corn, zucchini slices, red pepper pieces, and red onion slices with the olive oil and season with salt and pepper.
4. Place the vegetables on the grill and cook until all are starting to char.

5. Remove the vegetables from the grill. Remove the kernels of the corn by standing the ears upright and running a knife down the cob. Cut the remaining grilled vegetables into small half inch pieces.
6. Add all of the cut grilled vegetables to the cut romaine and toss with the vinaigrette. Garnish with the sunflower seeds and serve immediately.

Serves approximately 10 – 12 people as a side dish, or 4 to 6 as a meal.

Mediterranean Salad Dressing

"Dress your salad immediately after mixing, as this dressing will separate if left standing"

1/2 cup extra-virgin olive oil
1/4 cup balsamic vinegar
1/4 cup lemon juice
1/4 cup oil packed sundried tomatoes, drained & finely chopped
1 large garlic clove, crushed
2 tbsp liquid honey
1/2 tsp salt
1/2 tsp fresh cracked pepper

1. Place all ingredients in a bowl, and whisk thoroughly to combine. Pour immediately over your choice of greens.
2. Alternatively, place all ingredients in a glass jar with a lid, and shake thoroughly before serving.

Makes approximately 1.25 cups.

Mushroom Salad with Spicy Bacon Dressing

"Use any mixture of mushrooms that are available at your market - what I have listed here is my recommendation"

Salad

600g white button mushrooms, quartered
200g shitake mushrooms, stems removed & quartered
200g portabella mushrooms, roughly chopped
1 medium carrot, peeled & grated
1 green bell pepper, diced small
1 red bell pepper, diced small
4 green onions, sliced
1 handful fresh parsley, minced

Dressing

250g bacon slices, cooked crisp, drained and fat reserved
5 tbsp apple cider vinegar
3 tbsp Dijon mustard
5 tsp sambal oelek
2 tsp liquid honey
2 tsp anchovy paste, or two anchovies
1 garlic clove, crushed
1 tsp salt
1/2 tsp fresh cracked pepper
1 cup olive oil

1. Place all the salad ingredients in a large mixing bowl.
2. In a food processor, process the crisp bacon into fine bits, approximately 30 seconds on high.
3. Scrape down the sides of the food processor. Add 2 tablespoons of the reserved bacon fat and the remaining dressing ingredients except for the olive oil.
4. Turn the processor on high and drizzle the olive oil slowly into the moving mixture. Once the oil has been added, continue to puree on high for approximately 30 seconds to one minute.

5. Toss the dressing thoroughly into the salad ingredients and serve immediately.

Makes 8 - 12 portions as a side dish

Pumpkin Vinaigrette

"Great on greens with roasted pumpkin seeds and dried cranberries"

3/4 cup pumpkin puree
1/4 cup apple cider vinegar
2 tbsp maple syrup
1 tbsp molasses
1 tbsp Dijon or grainy mustard
3/4 tsp salt
1/2 tsp dried thyme leaves
1/4 tsp ground cinnamon
1/4 tsp ground nutmeg
1/4 tsp pepper
3/4 cup extra virgin olive oil

1. Mix all the ingredients, except for the oil, together in a bowl or food processor.
2. While continually mixing (or processing) slowly add the olive oil in a thin stream until completely blended.

Makes approximately 2 cups

South-Western Steak Salad

"Makes 4 large dinner sized salads"

Steak

2 tbsp paprika
1 tsp black pepper
1 tsp dried oregano
1 tsp salt
1/2 - 1 tsp cayenne pepper
1 – 700g beef flank steak
4 tbsp butter, melted
1 garlic clove, finely crushed or minced
1 tsp finely chopped parsley

Dressing

2 large soft avocados
Juice of 1 lime
1 cup sour cream
1/2 cup salsa
2 tsp chilli powder
2 tsp salt

Salad

1 large head Romaine lettuce, cut, washed, & dried
1 – 398ml can black beans, rinsed & drained
1 medium zucchini, quartered lengthwise & sliced
Kernels from 2 ears of fresh corn
1 large red bell pepper, diced small

1. In a small bowl, combine the paprika, pepper, oregano, salt, and cayenne. Liberally coat the steak with this mixture and let sit in the refrigerator for at least 1 hour. Mix the butter, garlic and parsley and set aside.
2. Preheat BBQ grill on high heat. Cook the flank steak for approximately 5 – 7 minutes per side, with the lid open, over medium-high heat for medium-rare to medium doneness – depending on the thickness of the

steak. When done, let rest for at least 3 to 5 minutes before slicing to help retain the juiciness of the meat.

3. While the steak is cooking, slice, pit and peel the avocados into a bowl large enough to make the dressing in. Mash the avocados with the lime juice as soon as possible to help prevent the avocado from oxidizing (turning brown). Mix in the sour cream, salsa, chilli powder, and salt to make the dressing.

4. Prepare 4 large bowls by equally portioning out the following ingredients in this order: Romaine, beans, zucchini, corn, and bell pepper.

5. Top each salad with an equal amount of dressing. Slice the rested steak thinly across the grain and place an equal amount of steak on each salad. Drizzle the meat with the reserved garlic butter and present to your guests... allowing them to admire the display before tossing the salad themselves.

Quick & Easy Oil & Vinegar Salad Dressing

"Why buy pre-made bottled oil & vinegar dressing, when you can make this in minutes?"

1/2 cup extra virgin olive oil
1/4 - 1/3 cup balsamic vinegar
1 tbsp liquid honey
1/2 tsp dried basil leaves
1/2 tsp dried oregano leaves
1/2 tsp salt
1/4 tsp fresh cracked pepper
1 garlic clove, finely crushed or minced

1. Put all ingredients in a jar with a lid and shake to combine, or mix thoroughly in a bowl.
2. Pour immediately over salad greens of your choice.

Makes slightly more than 3/4 cup

Warm Bacon Dressing

"The greens you dress this on will get a bit wilted, so only dress them immediately before serving"

Rendered fat from 1/2 pound bacon, approximately 1/2 cup
3 tbsp apple cider vinegar
1 to 2 tbsp maple syrup
2 tsp Dijon or grainy mustard
1/2 tsp dried thyme leaves
Fresh cracked pepper, to season

1. Add all the ingredients to the rendered bacon fat (make sure that the bacon fat is not too hot or the hot fat will splatter you when you add these ingredients).
2. Heat over medium heat until very warm while stirring together.
3. Serve immediately over your choice of greens (mixed greens or spinach leaves are fantastic).

RECIPE NOTES

SAUCES

Beurre Blanc

Brandied Cranberry Sauce

Garlic Tarragon Cream Sauce

Dez's Famous 4-Hour Gravy

Guinness Cream Sauce

Parsley Pesto

Salsa Verde

Beurre Blanc

"Beurre Blanc is a French term for White Butter Sauce. Excellent on fish or vegetables!

2 shallots, minced
1/4 cup white wine
2 tbsp white wine vinegar
2-3 tbsp whipping cream
1/2 cup cold butter, cubed into small pieces
Salt & fresh cracked pepper, to taste

1. Add shallots, wine and vinegar to a medium size pan and place over high heat. Bring to a boil and reduce the liquid in the pan to one tablespoon.
2. Stir in the whipping cream.
3. Reduce the heat to very low and start whisking the mixture while adding the cold butter pieces one at a time. Make sure that the butter is melting slowly so you can whisk it into a sauce consistency – if it melts too quickly it will just be a greasy mess. If it is melting too quickly, remove the pan from the heat for a minute or two and whisk it constantly before returning it to the low heat to continue whisking in the remaining butter. The addition of the cream in the previous step will act as a stabilizer to help you to whip air into the butter to become a sauce.
4. When all the butter has been incorporated, season to taste with salt & pepper and serve immediately.

Brandied Cranberry Sauce

"Very intense flavour – a homemade cranberry sauce to be proud of"

1 – 340g package fresh cranberries (approximately 3.5 cups)
1/2 cup packed dark brown sugar
1/2 cup brandy
2 cinnamon sticks, broken in half
zest of 1 lemon, finely chopped
pinch of salt

1. Combine all ingredients in a heavy bottomed medium-sized pot. Turn heat to medium-high and bring to a boil uncovered.
2. Once boiling, reduce the heat to medium and continue to cook mixture for approximately 10 to 15 minutes until desired consistency is reached, while occasionally stirring and mashing berries with a wooden spoon.
3. Remove from the heat; transfer the sauce into a different container and cool in the refrigerator. Once cooled, remove the cinnamon sticks and serve.

Makes approximately 2 cups

Garlic Tarragon Cream Sauce

"Don't be intimidated by the amount of garlic in this recipe. As the garlic cloves cook while the wine and broth reduces, they become very sweet and caramelized."

2 heads of garlic, cloves peeled & left whole
1 cup white wine
1 cup chicken broth
2 cups 35% M.F. whipping cream
1 tsp salt
2 tsp fresh chopped tarragon

1. Put garlic cloves and wine in a heavy bottomed pot, and bring to a boil over medium heat.
2. Turn the heat down to medium/low and simmer until all the liquid has evaporated, stirring occasionally. **Be careful not to burn the garlic**.
3. Once all of the wine has evaporated, add the chicken broth and bring to a boil over medium heat.
4. Turn the heat down to medium/low and simmer until all the broth has evaporated, stirring occasionally. **Be careful not to burn the garlic**.
5. Add the cream and bring to a simmer. Turn down the heat to low and cook for 5 to 10 minutes to reduce, stirring occasionally.
6. Puree the mixture in a blender or food processor for 30 seconds until garlic cloves have blended into the cream.
7. Return the sauce to the pot. Add the salt and tarragon and warm over low heat for a few minutes, to infuse the tarragon flavour into the sauce.
8. Serve immediately with your favorite pasta or use as a complimenting sauce to any seafood or chicken dish.

Makes approximately 2.25 cups

Dez's Famous 4-Hour Gravy

"Don't be intimidated by the name – it's 4 hours of cooking time, not 4 hours of constant attention! Made from the slow caramelization process of vegetables. If you have a Sunday afternoon to spare, this gravy offers tons of flavour and well worth the effort"

2 medium carrots, sliced into 1/4 inch coins
2 celery stalks, sliced 1/4 inch
3 tbsp vegetable oil
1 medium onion, sliced thin
1/4 cup butter
6 tbsp flour
1/2 cup full-bodied red wine
2 cups concentrated canned beef broth, or vegetable broth
1 tsp sugar
1/2 tsp salt
1/4 tsp pepper

1. Add carrot, celery and 2 tbsp of the vegetable oil to a large heavy bottomed non-stick pan. Toss to coat in the oil and cook over low to medium-low heat for approximately 1.5 hours, stirring occasionally. The carrot and celery will shrink in size, become soft, and just start to caramelize. *DO NOT CROWD THE PAN – It is important to use a large enough pan otherwise the vegetables will just steam in their juices instead of caramelize. The secret is to slowly caramelize the vegetables without burning them.

2. Stir in the onion and the other tbsp of vegetable oil to the carrots and celery and continue to cook, stirring occasionally, for another approximate 1.5 hours – all of the vegetables will become almost all dark brown (caramelized).

3. Add the butter to the vegetables, let it melt, and stir in the flour. Cook for 45 more minutes, stirring occasionally. The flour will become a "nut brown" in colour.

4. Stir in the wine slowly. It will start to get extremely thick. Continue by slowly stirring in the undiluted broth while incorporating to ensure no lumps.

5. Increase the heat to medium or medium-high while stirring to bring to a boil. Boiling will activate the full thickening power of the flour.
6. Strain the mixture through a wire-mesh strainer while pushing as much liquid as possible from the cooked vegetables. Discard the cooked vegetables.
7. Season the gravy with the sugar, salt, and pepper. If it is too thick then add a bit more liquid broth.

Makes approximately 1.75 cups

Guinness Cream Sauce

"Fantastic on classic Irish Colcannon. Rich, flavourful and leaves a finishing taste of Guinness on the palate."

1.75 (one and three quarters) cups beef broth
3 tbsp cornstarch
3/4 cup Guinness beer
1/4 cup dark brown sugar
1 tsp salt
1/2 tsp pepper
2 garlic cloves, crushed
3/4 cup whipping cream

1. In a small bowl, mix 1/4 cup of the beef broth with the cornstarch. Set aside.
2. In a medium heavy-bottomed pot, combine the rest of the beef broth with the beer, sugar, salt, pepper, and garlic. Heat to boiling over medium-high heat. Once boiling, reduce the heat down to medium-low and simmer for 10 minutes.
3. Add the cream and cornstarch mixture and whisk to combine. Increase the heat to medium-high and continue whisking constantly until it comes to a full boil and thickens. Remove from heat and serve.

Makes approximately 3 cups

Parsley Pesto

"Pesto is traditionally made with basil, but parsley is more readily available and works extremely well in this recipe!"

2/3 cup roasted, salted cashews
1/2 cup extra virgin olive oil
1/2 cup grated Parmesan cheese
2 large garlic cloves, peeled
juice of a 1/2 lemon
1/2 tsp salt
1/2 tsp fresh cracked pepper
1 bunch fresh curly leaf parsley, large stems removed

1. In a food processor, grind the cashews on high speed for approximately 15 seconds.
2. Continue to process on high speed while slowly adding 1/4 cup of the olive oil through the top opening, and then process for another 30 seconds until mixture is almost completely smooth and liquid.
3. Turn off the processor. Add the cheese, garlic, lemon juice, salt, and pepper. Turn the processor back on and process on high speed while feeding the parsley through the top opening. When all of the parsley has been added, continue to process on high speed while slowly adding the remaining 1/4 cup of olive oil.
4. Turn off the processor, scrape down the sides, and process for another 10 to 15 seconds.
5. Toss with hot freshly cooked pasta of your choice, or use in a variety applications such as a pizza or bruscetta topping."

Makes approximately 1.5 cups

Salsa Verde

"Great on sandwiches, bruscetta, grilled chicken breast, grilled fish, or served with a cheese & cracker platter"

1 slice bread
1/4 cup sundried tomatoes, packed in oil, drained
1 large garlic clove, peeled
1 bunch fresh parsley, large stems removed
zest of 1 lime, finely chopped
juice from 1/2 lime
5 tbsp extra-virgin olive oil
1 tbsp capers, drained
1 tsp anchovy paste, or 1 anchovy filet
1 tsp sugar
1/2 tsp salt
1/2 tsp fresh cracked pepper
1/4 tsp sambal oelek

1. In a food processor, process the bread slice on high speed until fine crumbs are formed, approximately 15 to 30 seconds.
2. Add all of the remaining ingredients to the bread crumbs and process on high for approximately 30 seconds. Scrape down the sides of the processor, and process for another 30 seconds until smooth texture is formed.

Makes approximately 1 cup

Soups & Stews

Black Bean Soup

Rustic Italian Bread Soup

Butternut Squash & Coconut Soup

Chicken & Sausage Gumbo

Clam Chowder

Bacon & Cheddar Corn Chowder

Fat Free Sweet Potato Bisque

Grandma G's Potato Soup

Guinness Beef Stew

Grilled Meat Jambalaya

Hop'n Shrimp Gumbo

Italian Sausage & Gnocchi Soup

Mexican Prawn Soup

Minestrone

Mom's Cherry Soup

Mulligatawny Soup

Oven Roasted Tomato Soup

Quick & Thick 3 Bean Chilli

Black Bean Soup

"The cut sizes for the bacon and vegetables really doesn't matter too much as the whole soup is pureed with a hand blender anyway"

125g bacon slices, cut into smaller pieces
1 small onion, chopped
1 green bell pepper, chopped
1 large carrot, chopped
1 celery stalk, chopped
2 jalapenos, chopped – seeds & membrane removed for mild
3 to 4 garlic cloves, chopped
2 – 540ml cans of black beans, drained & rinsed
3 to 4 cups chicken stock
1 small bunch fresh cilantro, chopped (reserve some for garnish)
1 medium tomato, chopped
2 tsp ground cumin
1/2 cup premade salsa
Salt & Pepper to taste
1/2 cup sour cream, for garnish

1. Add the bacon pieces to a large heavy bottomed pot over medium high heat and cook until fat has been rendered from the bacon. Cooked but not necessarily crisp, stirring occasionally.
2. Turn the heat down to medium and add the diced onions, green peppers, carrots, celery, jalapenos, garlic, and some salt & pepper to the bacon and bacon fat. Cover and cook until the vegetables are mostly soft, approximately 5 to 7 minutes.
3. Add the black beans and 3 cups of the chicken stock.
4. Add the cilantro, tomatoes, cumin, and salsa. Puree with a hand blender until smooth. Use the remaining 1 cup of chicken stock to thin the soup to your desired consistency while pureeing. Season with salt and pepper to taste.
5. Heat to desired temperature and serve each bowl garnished with a dollop of sour cream and a sprig of cilantro

Makes approximately 10 cups

Rustic Italian Bread Soup

500g loaf of bread (Crusty Italian or Sour Dough), cut in large cubes
1/4 cup extra virgin olive oil
1 tsp dried basil
1 tsp dried oregano
1 tsp salt
A few grinds of black pepper

2 tbsp extra virgin olive oil
1 small/medium onion, diced small
4 garlic cloves, minced
Salt & pepper
1 – 796ml can of diced tomatoes
1 – 900ml tetra pack of vegetable broth
1/2 cup chopped fresh basil leaves
1 tsp white sugar
1/2 to 1 tsp salt
Parmiggiano Regianno cheese, grated or shaved, for garnish

1. Preheat oven to 450 degrees Fahrenheit. Toss the bread cubes with the 1/4 cup olive oil, dried basil, dried oregano, 1 tsp salt, and a few grinds of black pepper. Spread on a baking sheet and bake 10 to 15 minutes until golden (like large croutons). Set aside.
2. Heat a pot over medium heat. Add the 2 tbsp olive oil, onion, garlic, and a sprinkle of salt and pepper. Cook, while stirring occasionally, for 2 to 3 minutes until the onion & garlic are soft.
3. Add the can of diced tomatoes and cook for another 2 to 3 minutes over medium heat.
4. Add the vegetable broth and bring to a boil.
5. Remove from the heat and stir in the fresh basil, sugar, and salt.
6. Divide the baked bread cubes into 8 soup bowls. Ladle an equal amount of soup into each bowl over the bread cubes. Garnish with the Parmiggiano and serve immediately.

Makes 8 portions

Butternut Squash & Coconut Soup

"A great vegetarian soup!"

1 tbsp olive oil
1 medium onion, diced small
4-5cm long piece of ginger, peeled and cut in fine strips
1 butternut squash (about 1 kg), peeled and cut in 1/2 inch cubes
4 cups vegetable stock
1 - 400ml can of coconut milk
Salt & pepper to taste
Toasted pumpkin seeds
Fresh cilantro

1. Heat the olive oil in a large pan over medium heat, add the onion and ginger and cook until soft, approximately 2 to 3 minutes. Add the butternut squash and cook for about 2-3 more minutes. Then add the stock and bring to a boil over high heat. Reduce the heat and simmer for about 20 minutes until butternut squash is soft.
2. Add the coconut milk and puree with a handheld mixer until you get a very smooth soup. Season with salt and fresh cracked pepper to taste. Serve immediately garnished with toasted pumpkin seeds and fresh cilantro.

Makes approximately 2 litres (8 cups)

Chicken & Sausage Gumbo

"Frequent stirring of the roux (fat & flour) will help prevent it from burning. My version of a gumbo thickened with both roux and okra. The amount of salt you use will depend on how salty your chicken broth is."

1/2 cup canola oil or vegetable oil
1/2 cup flour
1 medium onion, diced small, approximately 1.5 cups
1 medium red bell pepper, diced small, approximately 1 cup
2 celery stalks, diced small, approximately 1 cup
1 – 300g package frozen okra, thawed & sliced into circles
2 tsp dried thyme leaves (not ground)
2 bay leaves
6 to 8 garlic cloves, chopped
454g smoked andouille sausage, sliced lengthwise in half, then sliced into small pieces
10 boneless/skinless chicken thighs, cut into bite sized chunks
1/2 cup white wine
4 cups chicken broth
3 tsp sugar
1 – 156ml can tomato paste
1/2 tsp pepper
1 to 2 tsp salt, to taste
Cooked rice
Optional: garnish with a sprig of fresh thyme

1. Heat a large heavy bottomed pot over medium-high heat. Add the oil and heat slightly. Stir in the flour and reduce the heat to medium or medium-low and stir frequently for 20-30 minutes until this mixture (called a roux, pronounced 'roo') has turned dark brown, resembling the colour of melted milk chocolate.
2. Stir in the onion, bell pepper, and celery. Turn up the heat to medium and cook for approximately 2 to 3 minutes, stirring occasionally. It will get extremely thick.
3. Stir in the okra, thyme, and bay leaves and cook for approximately 2 to 3 more minutes, stirring occasionally.

4. Stir in the garlic, sausage, chicken, and wine. Cook for 5 minutes, stirring constantly until the chicken has mostly cooked.
5. Stir in the broth, sugar, tomato paste, and pepper. Increase the heat to high and bring to a boil. Then simmer at a low boil, uncovered, for 30 minutes, stirring occasionally, until it has reduced and thickened.
6. Season to taste with the salt and serve immediately over cooked rice, with or without garnish.

Makes 6 to 8 portions

Clam Chowder

"Adding fresh tomatoes to this cream based soup gives this classic New England style chowder more flavour and colour"

2 large red skin potatoes, diced 1/2 inch
2 tbsp olive oil
1 tbsp butter
1 medium onion, diced small
4 cloves garlic, minced
1 large carrot, sliced thin
2 large celery stalks, sliced thin
2 tsp dried tarragon
1 tsp dried basil
2 bay leaves
4 to 5 tsp salt
3 tsp sugar
1.5 tsp pepper
1/2 tsp sambal oelek, optional
1/4 cup flour
2 – 142g cans clams, clams & liquid separated and set aside
2.5 (two & one half) cups milk
1.5 (one & one half) cups whipping cream
2 large tomatoes, diced 1/2 inch
1/4 cup chopped fresh parsley

1. Steam the diced potatoes for approximately 8 to 10 minutes – do not overcook. Set aside.
2. Over medium heat, add the oil and butter to a large pot. Once the butter has melted add the onion, garlic, carrot, celery, tarragon, basil, bay leaves, salt, sugar, pepper, and sambal oelek. Stir to coat, and then cover and cook for approximately 5 minutes, stirring once during this cooking time. This will 'sweat' the vegetables in their own juice, not brown them.
3. Remove the lid and stir in the flour. Cook for another 2 to 3 minutes to remove the starchy taste of the flour, stirring occasionally.

4. To avoid lumps, stir in the liquid from the cans of clams very slowly. Once added, follow with the milk and whipping cream. Once all the liquid has been combined add the reserved potatoes, reserved clams, and tomatoes. Turn heat to medium-low and continue to cook until the soup is hot and has thickened slightly, stirring frequently to avoid burning.

5. Remove the bay leaves and discard them. Stir in the parsley, and serve immediately.

Makes 6 to 8 portions.

Bacon & Cheddar Corn Chowder

"This full flavoured soup is fast, simple, and hearty! Great with big chunks of crusty bread for dipping!"

Part "A"
6 slices bacon, sliced 1/4 inch
Part "B"
1 medium onion, diced small
4 cloves garlic, minced
1 large carrot, sliced thin
2 large celery stalks, sliced thin
4 cups corn kernels
1 tbsp olive oil
1 tbsp butter
2 tsp dried tarragon
1 tsp dried oregano
4 tsp salt
1 tbsp sugar
1.5 tsp pepper, freshly cracked
1/2 tsp sambal oelek
Part "C"
2 large russet potatoes, peeled/diced 1/2 inch
Part "D"
1/4 cup flour
2 cups milk
2 cups heavy cream
1/2 red bell pepper, diced small
2 cups grated old cheddar
1/4 cup chopped fresh parsley
Plus more chopped parsley for garnish

1. Cook bacon in a large heavy bottomed pot over medium-high heat until crisp. Remove the bacon with a slotted spoon and reserve for garnish.
2. Add all the ingredients in Part B to the rendered bacon fat in the pot. Stir to combine and once the butter is melted, cover and turn the heat

down to medium to sweat the vegetables until soft, approximately 5 minutes – do not brown the vegetables.

3. Steam the diced potatoes for approximately 8 to 10 minutes – do not over cook.

4. After sweating the vegetables, remove the lid and stir in the flour. Cook for approximately 2 to 3 minutes to remove the starchy taste of the flour.

5. To avoid lumps, stir the milk in gradually to the flour/vegetable mixture, and add the heavy cream. Partially puree with a hand blender.

6. Add the steamed potatoes, diced bell pepper, and <u>1 cup</u> of the grated cheddar. Bring to a simmer over medium heat, stirring frequently to avoid burning. Stir in 1/4 cup of parsley.

7. Garnish each bowl with the remaining grated cheddar, chopped parsley, and the reserved bacon pieces.

Makes 6 to 8 servings

Fat Free Sweet Potato Bisque

"This soup is so rich from the sweet potato it will seem like it has cream in it, but there is no added fat whatsoever! Not really a bisque, as that would involve cream – but it sounds better than Yam Soup."

1kg orange sweet potato, peeled, diced 1cm
1 tbsp dark brown sugar
1 tbsp salt
1/2 tsp ground nutmeg
1/4 tsp ground cloves
1/4 tsp ground white pepper
3.5 cups skim milk (or more)

For Garnish
1/4 cup no-fat sour cream
1 tbsp skim milk
Fresh parsley, finely chopped

1. Steam the diced sweet potato over boiling water for 20 minutes until fully cooked and tender.
2. Discard the water, and place the cooked sweet potato into a heavy bottomed pot, off the heat.
3. Add the brown sugar, salt, nutmeg, cloves, and white pepper to the sweet potato and combine thoroughly with a potato masher, ensuring no lumps.
4. Once fully mashed, start adding 1.5 cups of the skim milk slowly while continuing to mash with the potato masher. Switch to a whisk, turn the heat to medium, and blend in the remaining 2 cups of skim milk, mixing thoroughly until you have reached the consistency you like – you may need to add a bit more milk.
5. Stir occasionally over medium heat until completely heated through. Taste and adjust the seasonings if necessary.
6. While soup is heating, combine the sour cream with the tablespoon of milk.

7. Portion the soup into bowls and drizzle small amounts of the sour cream mixture on each portion. Drag a toothpick back and forth across the surface to create a beautiful design.
8. Sprinkle with chopped parsley and serve immediately.

Makes approximately 6 portions as a first course

Grandma G's Potato Soup

"Another classic recipe from my Grandma. This is one of my Mom's childhood favorites"

1/4 pound bacon, cut into 1/4 inch pieces
1 small onion, diced
3-4 stalks of celery, sliced (including the leaves)
2 tbsp finely chopped parsley
Salt & pepper
3 tbsp flour
1 cup chicken stock
5 cups water
4 medium potatoes, diced ½ inch, not peeled
1 cup cream
1 cup milk
Salt & pepper to taste
More finely chopped parsley for garnish

1. Sauté the bacon pieces in a heavy bottomed pot over medium heat until crisp.
2. Add the onion, celery, and parsley and season with salt & pepper, and sauté for another 10 minutes.
3. Add the flour and stir until a smooth paste forms; cooking for about two minutes.
4. Gradually add the chicken stock & water while stirring to prevent lumps.
5. Add the potatoes and bring to a slow boil. Turn the heat to low and simmer for approximately 1/2 hour until potatoes are tender.
6. Take a potato masher and mash the potatoes into the soup – do not mash too much as you still want some texture.
7. Add the cream and milk and cook over low heat until hot, stirring occasionally.
8. Season to taste with salt and pepper. Garnish with parsley.

Guinness Beef Stew

4 tbsp canola oil
1 kg cubed beef chuck stewing meat
Salt & pepper
4 medium carrots, 1/2 to 3/4 inch coins
2 celery stalks, sliced
1 medium onion, diced small
6 garlic cloves, chopped small
2 stalks fresh rosemary, chopped
3 bay leaves
1 – 440ml can of Guinness beer
1 cup full bodied red wine
1 cup beef broth
2 tbsp dark brown sugar
2 large red-skinned potatoes, diced 1/2 to 3/4 inch
2 tbsp cornstarch with a few tbsp red wine, optional

1. Heat a heavy bottomed large pot over medium high heat.
2. Toss the stew meat with 1 tablespoon of the oil and salt & pepper.
3. Add the other 3 tablespoons of oil to the heated pot. Brown the stew pieces in the hot oil – making sure not to overcrowd the pot. As the pieces are browned, remove and set aside.
4. Lower the heat to medium and add the carrot, celery, onion, garlic, rosemary and more salt & pepper. Cook for approximately 2 minutes until the vegetables have softened a bit.
5. Add the bay leaves, Guinness, wine, broth, brown sugar, potatoes, and the reserved browned stew meat. Bring to a boil and then cover, reduce the heat to low and simmer for 1.5 to 2 hours until the meat is tender. Season to taste with salt & pepper and serve.
6. **Optional – if you want a thicker broth – mix the cornstarch with the few tablespoons of wine and stir it into the finished stew. Bring to a boil to thicken and then serve.

Makes 6 to 8 portions

Grilled Meat Jambalaya

"Grilling the meat brings extra flavor to this classic Mardi Gras dish"

2 tsp canola oil
1 medium onion, diced small
1 medium red bell pepper, diced small
1 celery stalk, diced small
6 garlic cloves, minced
1/2 tsp salt
1 & 1/2 cups long grain white rice
1 - 284ml can condensed chicken broth
1 - 240ml bottle clam juice
1 – 398ml can diced tomatoes, not drained
1 tsp dried thyme leaves
2 bay leaves
2 tsp sugar
1 tsp ground cayenne pepper
4 boneless skinless chicken thighs
Canola oil
Salt & pepper
200g smoked (pre-cooked) chorizo sausage
454g (1 pound) cooked large shrimp
Fresh parsley, chopped for garnish

1. Heat a heavy bottomed pot over medium heat.
2. Add the oil and then the onion, bell pepper, celery, garlic, and salt. Stir to combine and cook until soft, approximately 2 – 3 minutes stirring occasionally.
3. Add the rice, condensed broth, clam juice, tomatoes, thyme, bay leaves, sugar, and cayenne. Stir to combine. Turn the heat to high and bring to a boil.
4. Cover, reduce the heat to low, and simmer for 20 minutes.
5. Keep the pot covered, remove from the heat and let stand for 5 minutes.
6. **While the rice mixture is cooking, prepare and grill the chicken and sausage as follows:**

7. Oil the chicken thighs and season with salt and pepper. Grill for approximately 7 – 8 minutes per side over medium high heat until cooked through. Grill the whole sausages over lower heat until the outside is slightly charred. Chorizo sausages are usually pre-cooked when you buy them (check with your deli), so this is just to get more of a flame-licked smoky flavour to them.
8. Remove the chicken and sausage from the grill and let stand a few minutes. Cut the chicken and sausage into "bite-sized" pieces.
9. Remove the bay leaves from the rice mixture and stir in the grilled meats. Then stir in the cooked shrimp and serve immediately, garnished with the chopped parsley. (Since the shrimp is already cooked it is added last to just warm them through without overcooking them. Overcooked shrimp have a rubber-like texture.)

Makes 4 to 6 servings.

Hop'n Shrimp Gumbo

"Classic 'no roux' gumbo made with beer and shrimp. The okra adds body to this wonderful New Orleans style soup. Fresh okra is better if you can get it."

3 tbsp olive oil
2 large celery stalks, diced small
1 large red bell pepper, diced small
1 medium-large onion, diced small
6 garlic cloves, minced
2 tsp paprika
2 tsp sugar
1.5 tsp dried thyme leaves
1 tsp salt
1/2 tsp pepper
1/2 tsp ground cayenne pepper
250g fresh or thawed frozen okra, sliced into 1/4 inch rings
2 – 355ml cans of beer
1 – 284ml can condensed chicken broth
1/2 cup dry orzo pasta
Juice of 1 lemon
454g (1 pound) cooked small shrimp
Fresh thyme sprigs, for garnish
Zest of 1 lemon

1. Heat a heavy bottomed pot over medium heat.
2. Add the oil and then the celery, bell pepper, onion, garlic, paprika, sugar, dried thyme, salt, pepper, and cayenne pepper. Cook for 2 – 3 minutes until soft, stirring occasionally.
3. Add the okra and continue to cook for 2 – 3 minutes until the okra starts to get sticky.
4. Slowly stir in the beer. Stir in the condensed chicken broth. Turn the heat to high and bring to a boil.
5. Stir in the orzo pasta and simmer uncovered over medium-low heat for approximately 6 – 8 minutes until the pasta is cooked.

6. Remove from the heat and stir in the lemon juice and the shrimp and serve immediately, with each bowl garnished with a fresh thyme sprig and lemon zest.

Makes 6-8 servings

Italian Sausage & Gnocchi Soup

500g mild Italian sausage, casings removed and discarded
1 tbsp olive oil
6 garlic cloves, minced
1/2 cup finely chopped onion
1.5 tsp salt
1/2 tsp pepper
1 – 796ml can of diced tomatoes
2 – 900ml chicken broth
1 tsp sugar
1 – 500g package of potato gnocchi pasta
1 packed cup fresh baby spinach leaves
1/4 cup thinly sliced fresh basil
Generous amounts of shaved Pecorino Romano cheese

1. Add the sausage meat, olive oil, garlic, onion, salt and pepper to a large pot. Turn the heat to medium and cook for approximately 5 to 7 minutes until the sausage in cooked through, while breaking up the sausage meat with a spoon as it cooks.
2. Add the can of tomatoes, chicken broth, and sugar. Increase the heat to medium high to bring to a boil. Once boiling, add the gnocchi and continue to cook for 3 minutes.
3. Remove the pot from the heat. Stir in the spinach and basil and portion out immediately; garnished with generous amounts of shaved Pecorino Romano cheese.

Makes approximately 13 cups

Mexican Prawn Soup

"A great Mexican inspired soup. The crushed tortilla shells become part of the body of the soup and help to season it as well."

2 tbsp canola oil
1 small onion, chopped
1 carrot, sliced thin
2 celery stalks, chopped
6 garlic cloves, chopped
1 chopped jalapeno, seeds & membrane removed
1 whole canned chipotle pepper
1 tsp dried oregano
1 tsp salt
1/2 tsp pepper
454g (1 pound) raw Black Tiger Prawns, shells removed and reserved, prawn meat reserved
1 cup white wine
3 tbsp tomato paste (approx. 1/2 of a156ml can)
4 cups vegetable stock
1 tbsp sugar
Juice of 1/2 lime
1/2 cup finely chopped cilantro
Garnish with crumbled salted tortilla chips, dollops of sour cream, and small diced red bell pepper

1. Heat a pot over medium heat. Add the oil, followed by the onion, carrot, celery, garlic, jalapeno, chipotle, oregano, salt, and pepper. Stir to combine and then cover with a lid. Cook for 3 to 4 minutes until the vegetables are soft.
2. Remove this cooked vegetable mixture and set aside.
3. Add the reserved prawn shells to the pot along with the white wine. Bring to a boil over the medium heat and then cover with a lid. Cook for 3 to 4 minutes. This will release incredible prawn flavour from the shells.
4. Place these cooked shells in a fine wire strainer over a bowl and shake and stir to get all the liquid from the shells. Once this is done, discard

the shells and add the extracted liquid back to the pot along with the reserved vegetables from step 2.

5. Stir in the tomato paste, vegetable stock, and the sugar. Puree in the pot with a handheld blender (a food processor or regular blender can be used instead and then transfer back to the pot, but you may have to do it in batches to prevent it overflowing).

6. Cut the prawn meat into smaller pieces (halves or thirds) and add them to the pot. Bring to a full boil over medium-high heat, while stirring occasionally, to cook the prawns.

7. Remove from the heat and stir in the lime juice and the cilantro. Serve immediately in bowls garnished with crushed tortilla chips, sour cream, and small diced red bell pepper.

Makes approximately 7 cups

Minestrone

"Classic Italian vegetable soup at its finest! Make sure to cut all the vegetables in small uniform sizes for attractiveness and variety in each spoonful. Pancetta (Italian bacon) would be more classic, but I prefer the smokiness of regular bacon in this recipe."

250g bacon slices, sliced into 1/4 inch pieces
1 medium onion, diced 1/4 inch
1 medium carrot, diced 1/4 inch
2 celery stalks, diced 1/4 inch
6 garlic cloves, minced
1/2 tsp salt
1/4 tsp pepper
2 stalks fresh rosemary, chopped
1 chunk of parmesan rind
1 cup white wine
1 – 796ml can diced tomatoes
4 cups vegetable broth
3 bay leaves
1.5 cups of 1/4 inch diced butternut squash
1 small zucchini, diced 1/4 inch, approximately 2 cups
3/4 cup dry orzo pasta
1 – 540ml can Romano beans or kidney beans, drained & rinsed
1.5 tsp sugar
1/4 cup chopped fresh parsley
Salt & pepper to season
Parmigiano Reggiano cheese, shaved for garnish

1. In a large pot over medium/high heat, cook the bacon pieces until crisp, stirring occasionally. Remove with a slotted spoon and set aside while leaving the rendered bacon fat in the pan.
2. Turn the heat to medium and add the onion, carrot, celery, garlic, salt, pepper, rosemary and cook for approximately 2 to 3 minutes until softened a bit, stirring occasionally.
3. Add the parmesan rind, wine, tomatoes, 4 cups of the broth, bay leaves, squash, and zucchini.

4. Turn the heat to high and bring to a boil. Add the orzo, reduce the heat to medium/high and continue to cook uncovered until the orzo has cooked to al dente, approximately 6 to 8 minutes, stirring occasionally.
5. Remove from the heat and add the beans, sugar and parsley. Season to taste with salt and pepper, and remove & discard the parmesan rind and bay leaves.
6. Garnish each bowl with shavings of Parmigiano Reggiano and the reserved bacon pieces.

Makes approximately 3 litres

Mom's Cherry Soup

"My Mom used to make this every summer during cherry season when I was a child. It is one of the many great memories I have. When my Mom was a child, my Grandma used to make it for her and her siblings. In those days, my Grandpa would go to town and bring home just one basket of cherries, because that was all that they could afford. Since there were so many kids, one basket of cherries wouldn't go very far. Grandma came up with this recipe of cherry soup so that they would all get their share of the cherries."

1 pound fresh cherries (approx 3 cups), left whole, stems removed
4 cups + 2 tbsp water
1 cup + 1/4 cup sugar
3/4 cup flour
1/4 tsp salt

1. Wash the cherries and place them in a medium sized pot. Add the 4 cups water and 1 cup of the sugar. Bring to a boil over medium-high heat.
2. In a bowl, mix the flour, 1/4 cup sugar, and salt together. Add the 2 tbsp water and stir with a fork until the flour mixture is moist. Then with your fingers work the flour mixture to make little "flour curds" and set aside.
3. When cherries have come to a boil, add the curds a small handful at a time. When the curds have all been added, reduce the heat to medium and boil for 5 more minutes, stirring occasionally.
4. Serve hot or at room temperature.

Makes approximately 4 to 6 servings.

Photo Credit: Beverly Hudson

Mulligatawny Soup

1/4 cup butter
1 medium onion, diced small
2 celery stalks, diced small
1 medium carrot, diced small
6 garlic cloves, minced
2 tbsp flour
2 tsp curry powder
1 tsp garam masala
1/4 tsp dried thyme
4 cups chicken broth/stock
1/4 cup dried green lentils
2 bay leaves
1 apple, peeled and diced
2 cooked chicken breasts, cubed (preferably grilled)
1 – 400ml can of coconut milk
1.5 tsp salt
1/2 tsp pepper

1. Add butter to a pot over medium heat. Once the butter foams, add the onion, celery, carrot, and garlic. Stir to combine and cook for 2 to 3 minutes stirring occasionally until soft.
2. Add the flour, curry powder, garam masala, and thyme and cook for 2 to 3 more minutes, stirring frequently.
3. Slowly add the chicken broth and stir to combine while adding to prevent lumps. Add the lentils and bay leaves. Bring to a boil and then simmer over low heat uncovered for 30 minutes, stirring occasionally.
4. Stir in the apple, chicken, and coconut milk. Continue to simmer for another 10 to 15 minutes to ensure that the lentils are cooked and to let the flavours come together.
5. Season with the salt and pepper, discard the bay leaves, and serve immediately.

Makes approximately 8 cups

Oven Roasted Tomato Soup

"If you love tomato soup, but not all of the fat that is in traditional tomato cream soup, you will love this recipe! Roasting all of the vegetables really brings out the flavour. If you don't have an immersion hand-blender, then a food processor or blender will work as well."

1kg ripe Roma tomatoes
1 head of garlic, peeled, cloves separated and left whole
1 small-medium onion, rough chopped
2 tbsp olive oil
2 tbsp balsamic vinegar
1 tbsp dried oregano leaves
1 tbsp dried basil leaves
1 tsp white sugar
Salt and fresh cracked pepper
2 cups of chicken stock

1. Preheat oven to 450 degrees.
2. Cut Roma tomatoes in half lengthwise.
3. In a large bowl toss the tomato halves, garlic and onion with the oil, vinegar, oregano, basil, sugar, and season with salt and pepper.
4. Empty this mixture onto a large baking sheet and arrange the tomatoes cut-side down. If the baking sheet is too crowded you may want to roast them in two batches – over crowding will prevent the vegetable from caramelizing as much as they should.
5. Bake for approximately 35 to 40 minutes until the vegetables are cooked and caramelized.
6. Transfer these ingredients to a large pot, add the chicken stock and puree with an immersion hand-blender. Bring to desired temperature over medium heat while stirring occasionally. Re-season to taste with salt, pepper and sugar.
7. Serve immediately.

Makes approximately 4 to 5 cups

Quick & Thick 3 Bean Chili

1 pound lean ground beef
3 tbsp & 1 tsp chili powder
1 tbsp dried oregano
1 tbsp ground cumin
1 tbsp olive oil
2 tsp salt
1 tsp ground cayenne pepper
1 tsp black pepper
1 medium onion, chopped
4 garlic cloves, chopped
1 - 398ml can of refried beans
2 cups frozen corn kernels
1 796ml can of diced tomatoes – do not drain
1 398ml can of red kidney beans, drained & rinsed
1 540ml can of black beans, drained & rinsed
3 tbsp dark brown sugar
2 tsp beef stock paste
1/2 cup dark beer
1 cup grated cheddar cheese, for garnish
1 cup sour cream, for garnish
chopped parsley, for garnish (optional)

1. Add the beef, chili powder, oregano, cumin, oil, salt, cayenne, pepper, onion, and garlic to a large heavy bottomed pot.
2. Turn the heat to medium high while mixing thoroughly until the beef is completely cooked.
3. Remove from the heat and incorporate the can of refried beans until it is thoroughly combined.
4. Place the pot back on the heat and add all of the remaining ingredients (except the cheese, sour cream, and parsley), and stir occasionally until it is completely heated through.
5. Serve in bowls with a sprinkle of cheddar, a dollop of sour cream, and a light sprinkling of parsley.

Makes 6 to 8 servings

PASTA

Dez's Famous Sausage & Fennel Pasta

Lamb Pasta Sauce

Linguine Puttanesca

Pasta with Butter, Garlic, & Cheese

Tomato Pasta Sauce

Tomato Rosé Pasta Sauce

Dez's Famous Sausage & Fennel Pasta

3 tbsp olive oil
500g mild Italian sausage, casings removed
1 medium onion, diced very small
4 - 6 large cloves of garlic, minced
2 tbsp fennel seed
1 tsp salt
A few grinds of black pepper
1 – 156ml can tomato paste
1 – 796ml can of diced tomatoes
1 cup of full-bodied red wine
1 tsp vegetable stock paste
2 tbsp white sugar
1/2 tsp sambal oelek, optional**
400g penne pasta or other favourite pasta shape
1 cup whipping cream
Chopped fresh parsley, for garnish
Grated Parmigiano Reggiano cheese, for garnish

1. Add the olive oil, sausage, onion, garlic, fennel seed, salt and pepper to a large heavy bottomed pan.
2. Turn the heat on to medium-high and cook, while breaking up the sausage, until the sausage is fully cooked and in small pieces, approximately 8 to 12 minutes.
3. Stir in the tomato paste, diced tomatoes, wine, vegetable paste, sugar, and sambal oelek. Bring to a boil and reduce over medium heat until the sauce becomes very thick, approximately 10 to 15 minutes. Cook your pasta in boiling, liberally salted water to desired consistency (approximately 13 to 15 minutes for penne) during this step.
4. Once the sauce has reduced, stir in the whipping cream and then the cooked and drained pasta. Serve immediately garnished with parsley and grated Parmigiano Reggiano.

Makes approximately 6 portions

Lamb Pasta Sauce

"A pasta sauce for lamb lovers!"

500g lean ground lamb
2 tbsp extra virgin olive oil
1 small onion, diced small
1 carrot, diced small
1 celery stalk, diced small
10 to 15 juniper berries, optional
3 garlic cloves, chopped
1 to 2 fresh rosemary sprigs, stems discarded
1.5 tsp salt
1/2 tsp pepper
1/2 cup full-bodied red wine, or low-sodium beef broth
2 bay leaves
500g pasta shapes, like penne, rigatoni, etc, cooked as desired
Chopped fresh parsley for garnish

1. Add the lamb, oil, onion, carrot, celery, juniper berries, garlic, rosemary, salt and pepper to a large pan. Cook over medium heat until the lamb is cooked through, stirring occasionally and breaking up the lamb as it cooks, approximately 10 minutes.
2. Stir in the red wine (or low-sodium beef broth) and the bay leaves. Bring to a boil and then cover, reduce the heat to low and simmer covered for 1 hour.
3. Remove and discard the bay leaves. Pulse the cooked sauce in a blender (or food processor) until a smooth consistency is reached. Re-season to taste with salt & pepper if necessary.
4. Serve immediately on the freshly cooked pasta and garnish with chopped parsley.

Makes approximately 3.5 cups of sauce, or 4 to 6 portions with the cooked pasta

Linguine Puttanesca

"Linguine Puttanesca (pronounced "ling-gweenee poo-tan-ness-ka") is a classic dish from old world Italy. Rumors indicates that Italian "working women" created this dish as a quick meal to prepare between visits with clients."

2 – 3 tbsp olive oil
1 tsp dried crushed chilies
2 cloves garlic, minced
2 tsp anchovy paste, or 2 anchovy filets
1 – 796ml can of diced tomatoes, drained
2 tbsp red or white wine (optional)
1/2 cup pitted & halved kalamata olives, firmly packed
2 tbsp capers, drained
3/4 cup chopped fresh parsley, loosely packed
300g dry linguine, cooked al denté
Salt & fresh cracked pepper to season

1. Add the oil, chilies, garlic and anchovy to a large pan and heat over medium-low heat to infuse the flavours – approximately 3-5 minutes. Be careful not to burn the garlic.
2. Add the drained tomatoes and the wine (optional) and increase the heat to medium-high. Boil until reduced – approximately 4-5 minutes. Stirring occasionally.
3. Remove from the heat. Toss in the olives, capers, parsley and hot cooked pasta.
4. Season to taste with salt and pepper and serve immediately.

Makes approximately 4 portions

Pasta with Butter, Garlic, & Cheese

"Probably one of the simplest side pasta dishes"

1/3 (one third) cup butter
3 to 4 garlic cloves, finely crushed or minced
250g dry linguine
1/2 cup grated parmesan or romano cheese
Salt & fresh cracked pepper
1 small handful of parsley, chopped fine

1. Place a large pan over low heat. Add the butter and the crushed garlic cloves. Let the butter melt and get infused with the garlic. Do not increase the temperature of the pan to ensure not burning the garlic or butter. Put a large pot of salted water on high heat to bring to a boil in the meantime.
2. Once the water is boiling cook the dry linguine for approximately 8 minutes, or until desired consistency is reached.
3. Drain the cooked pasta and shake thoroughly to rid it of as much excess water as possible. Add to the melted butter and toss with the cheese.
4. Season to taste with salt and fresh cracked pepper and garnish with the chopped parsley.

Makes 4 to 6 side portions

Tomato Pasta Sauce

"Never buy pre-made store bought pasta sauce again. Suitable for freezing - for pasta sauce at a moment's notice."

3 tbsp olive oil
1 medium/large carrot, diced very small
2 large celery stalks, diced very small
1 medium onion, diced very small
6 cloves of garlic, minced
1 tbsp dried oregano
2 tsp dried basil
salt & pepper
1 – 156ml can tomato paste
1 – 796ml can of diced tomatoes
1 cup of full-bodied red wine
1 cup vegetable broth, or 1 tsp vegetable paste
2 tbsp white sugar
1/2 tsp sambal oelek
salt & fresh cracked pepper to taste
fresh parsley, for garnish
grated Parmesan cheese, for garnish

1. Heat a large heavy bottomed pot over medium to medium-high heat.
2. Add the olive oil.
3. Add carrot, celery, onion, garlic, oregano, and basil. Gently season with salt & pepper, and cook until soft but not brown, about 3 - 5 minutes; stirring frequently.
4. Stir in the tomato paste.
5. Stir in the can of tomatoes (not drained), wine, vegetable broth, sugar, and sambal oelek.
6. Bring to a boil. Reduce until desired consistency is reached; stirring occasionally; approximately 5 – 10 minutes.
7. Season to taste and serve with your favorite pasta and garnish with freshly chopped parsley and grated parmesan cheese.

Makes approximately 6 cups

Tomato Rosé Pasta Sauce

"With the addition of cream, this tomato sauce becomes rich & irresistible"

3 tbsp olive oil
1 medium/large carrot, diced very small
2 large celery stalks, diced very small
1 medium onion, diced very small
6 cloves of garlic, minced
1 tbsp dried oregano
2 tsp dried basil
salt & pepper
1 – 156ml can tomato paste
1 – 796ml can of diced tomatoes
1 cup of full-bodied red wine
1 cup vegetable broth, or 1 tsp vegetable paste
2 tbsp white sugar
1/2 tsp sambal oelek
1/2 – 3/4 cup 35% whipping cream
salt & fresh cracked pepper to taste
fresh parsley, for garnish
grated parmesan cheese, for garnish

1. Heat a large heavy bottomed pot over medium to medium-high heat.
2. Add the olive oil.
3. Add carrot, celery, onion, garlic, oregano, and basil. Gently season with salt & pepper, and cook until soft but not brown, about 3 - 5 minutes; stirring frequently.
4. Stir in the tomato paste.
5. Stir in the can of tomatoes (not drained), wine, vegetable broth, sugar, and sambal oelek.
6. Bring to a boil and reduce until liquid almost gone; watching closely and stirring frequently; approximately 10 – 15 minutes. Stir in the cream and remove from the heat.
7. Season to taste and serve with your favorite pasta and garnish with freshly chopped parsley and grated parmesan cheese.

Makes approximately 6.5 cups

RECIPE NOTES

BEEF & LAMB

Beef & Broccoli Stir-Fry

Beef Barley Slow-Cooker Stew

Beef Grilling Rub

Jus

Cajun Grilled Flank Steak with Grits

Greek Lamb Burgers

Greek Souvlaki

Mozza Stuffed Hamburgers

Grilled Philly Cheesesteaks

Quick Meat Marinade

Guinness Shepherd's Pie

Pepper Steak Madagascar

Steaks with Merlot Reduction

Rack of Lamb with Blueberry Reduction

Southwestern Steak Diane

Stewed leg of Lamb

Maple & Bourbon Beef Short Ribs

Beef & Broccoli Stir-Fry

600g flank steak
Pepper
4 tbsp grape seed oil or canola oil
8 cups broccoli florets
1 small onion sliced thin
6 cloves garlic, minced
1 to 2 tbsp minced ginger
1/2 cup water
2 cups beef broth
1/2 cup oyster sauce
1/4 cup soy sauce
2.5 to 3 tbsp cornstarch mixed with the soy sauce above
Cooked rice or noodles, optional

1. Slice the flank steak into 3 equal pieces by cutting with the grain of the meat. Then slice each piece against the grain into thin slices. Season the beef slices with pepper.
2. Heat a large wok over high heat.
3. When hot, add 1 tbsp of the oil and sauté half of the beef until juices have evaporated and beef has browned. Remove the beef and set aside. Add another tbsp of oil and repeat with the second half of the beef and set aside.
4. Turn down the heat to medium-high and add the last 2 tbsp of oil. Immediately add the broccoli, onion, garlic, and ginger and sauté for only 30 seconds to ensure the garlic doesn't burn. Add the water and then cover to steam for 2 minutes.
5. Return the beef and any accumulated juices to the wok along with the beef broth, oyster sauce, and soy sauce/cornstarch mixture. Stir together and then move the beef and broccoli up the sides of the wok and boil the sauce in the middle until thickened. Stir everything back together and serve immediately with or without the optional rice/noodles.

Makes approximately 6 full portions

Beef Barley Slow-Cooker Stew

680g (1.5 pounds) beef stew meat
3 tbsp canola oil
Salt & pepper
2 medium onions, chopped
1 large carrot, sliced lengthwise, then into 1/2-inch pieces
2 celery stalks, sliced into 1/2-inch pieces
8 to 10 garlic cloves
3 tbsp apple juice or apple cider
8 medium mushrooms, quartered
2 to 3 tbsp chopped fresh rosemary
2 bay leaves
2 tsp beef stock paste
1/2 cup pearl barley
1 – 798ml can diced tomatoes
2 cups apple juice or apple cider

1. Preheat a large pan over medium-high heat. In a bowl toss beef pieces with 2 tablespoons of oil and season with salt and pepper. When the pan is hot, add the other tablespoon of oil to the pan and brown each piece of meat without crowding the pan – you may have to brown the beef in 2 or 3 batches. When each batch of meat is browned transfer to the slow-cooker.
2. Turn off the heat to the pan and add the onions, carrot, celery, garlic and the 3 tablespoons of apple cider to the pan. Stir until the pan has cooled and the vegetables have cooked slightly, approximately 1 to 2 minutes. Transfer this vegetable mixture to the slow-cooker.
3. To the slow-cooker add the mushrooms, rosemary, bay leaves, beef paste, barley, tomatoes (with juice) and the apple cider.
4. Turn the slow-cooker on low and cook for approximately 8 to 10 hours.
5. Remove and discard the bay leaves and season to taste with salt and pepper before serving.

Makes approximately 12 cups

Beef Grilling Rub
"A great basic spice rub for all beef destined for the BBQ"

4 tbsp sweet smoked paprika
2 tbsp dried granulated garlic
4 tsp salt
2 tsp ground black pepper
2 tsp dried thyme leaves
1/2 tsp ground cayenne pepper, optional

1. Mix together and thoroughly coat your choice of beef before grilling.

Makes approximately 1/2 cup

Jus
"The perfect broth dipping sauce for beef"

1 cup full bodied red wine
3 garlic cloves, peeled and cut in half
1 sprig fresh rosemary
1 cup beef broth
1/2 tsp salt
1/2 tsp sugar

1. Combine the red wine, garlic cloves, and rosemary in a small pot. Boil over medium/high to high heat until the wine has reduced in volume by half (one half cup). Add the beef stock, salt and sugar. Stir to combine, remove from the heat, cover and set aside until needed.

Makes 1.5 cups

Cajun Grilled Flank Steak with Grits

"Grits are traditionally made with ground Hominy, but since this is not readily available I have substituted it with fine cornmeal."

Steak
1/4 cup paprika
2 tsp ground black pepper
2 tsp ground dried oregano
2 tsp salt
1/2 - 1 tsp cayenne pepper
1 – 600g-700g beef flank steak

Garlic Butter (mix together)
4 tbsp melted butter
1 garlic clove, finely crushed or minced
1 tsp finely chopped parsley

Grits
2 cups water
2 tsp salt
2 cups milk
1/2 cup butter, cubed small
1 cup fine cornmeal
100g Montery Jack cheese, grated
2 garlic cloves, finely minced

1. In a small bowl, combine the paprika, pepper, oregano, salt, and cayenne. Liberally coat the steak with this mixture and let sit in the refrigerator for at least 1 hour.
2. Preheat BBQ grill. Cook the flank steak for approximately 5 – 7 minutes per side, over medium-high heat for medium-rare to medium doneness – depending on the thickness of the steak.
3. Let rest for 2 – 3 minutes before slicing to help retain the juiciness of the meat.
4. Once the steak has rested, slice the steak across the grain into thin strips.

5. Serve each plate with a dollop of grits topped with strips of flank steak and drizzled with 1 tablespoon of garlic butter.

<u>Prepare the grits while the steak is grilling:</u>
1. In a heavy bottomed pot, bring the water and salt to a boil over high heat.
2. Add the milk and butter and stir until the butter has melted into the liquid.
3. Turn the heat to low and add the cornmeal gradually while whisking.
4. Simmer, while whisking constantly, for approximately 3 – 5 minutes until mixture has thickened.
5. Stir in the cheese gradually and stir in the garlic.
6. Remove from heat, cover, and set aside until the steak is ready to serve.

Makes 4 to 6 servings

Greek Lamb Burgers

500g lean ground lamb (or ground beef, if preferred)
1 large egg
7 garlic cloves, finely minced
3 tbsp finely chopped fresh oregano
2 tbsp finely chopped fresh rosemary
1 tsp salt & 1/2 tsp pepper
100g feta cheese, crumbled

1. Mix all ingredients in a bowl and divide equally into four portions. Shape each portion into a burger patty.
2. On a preheated BBQ, grill the burgers over medium flame until cooked through or alternatively in a preheated pan over medium heat. Approximately 4 to 5 minutes per side but an instant read thermometer is the way to go: 71 degrees C or 160 degrees F.
3. Serve with Tzatziki, and lettuce, and optional tomato on your favourite burger buns.

Makes 4 burgers

Greek Souvlaki

"Chicken breast proteins are more fragile than red meat proteins, thus requires less marinating time – over marinated chicken will become tough."

1.5 to 2 pounds leg of lamb, approximately 1 inch cubes
OR
1.5 to 2 pounds beef stew meat, approximately 1 inch cubes
OR
1.5 to 2 pounds chicken breast filets

2/3 cup olive oil
1/3 cup fresh lemon juice
1 tbsp white wine vinegar
3 garlic cloves, finely crushed or minced
1 tbsp dried oregano (leaves, not ground)
2-3 bay leaves, crumbled
salt and pepper to season

1. Place lamb, beef or chicken in a large zip-lock bag.
2. Mix all other ingredients in a bowl, and pour into bag of lamb, beef or chicken.
3. Seal the bag leaving as little air as possible; toss around to coat.
4. Let marinate in fridge (24 hours for lamb/beef or 3 - 4 hours for chicken), tossing around occasionally.
5. If using wooden skewers, soak them in cold water for at least 24 hours to help prevent them from burning.
6. Put meat on skewers; the number of skewers you will need, will depend of the number of pieces you want to serve per portion.
7. Grill skewers over a medium to medium-high heat turning occasionally until done, approximately 10-20 minutes depending on the temperature of your grill.
8. Serve warm, still on skewers, on a bed of rice, and tzatziki for dipping.

Makes four to six servings.

Mozza Stuffed Hamburgers

"Loaded with flavour, these burgers will be the hit at your next barbeque"

1 kg (2.2 pounds) lean ground beef
8 garlic cloves, finely crushed or minced
1 egg
2/3 cup cornflake crumbs
1/2 cup minced onion
1/2 cup oil packed sundried tomatoes, drained & chopped
1/4 cup berry jam
1 tbsp salt
1 tbsp dried basil leaves
2 tsp sambal oelek
1 tsp dried thyme leaves
1 tsp chilli powder
1 tsp pepper
100g mozzarella cheese, cut into 8 small chunks

1. Mix all of the ingredients together (except for the mozzarella) in a large bowl.
2. Preheat your cooking surface; pan, grill, griddle, etc.
3. Portion the hamburger mixture into eight equal sized balls.
4. Flatten each ball in your hand and encase a chunk of mozzarella in the middle by shaping it into a large patty, by wrapping the meat around the cheese.
5. Over a medium heat/flame, cook the patties until thoroughly cooked through, approximately 8 to 12 minutes per side. Internal meat temperature should be 160 degrees Fahrenheit or 71 degrees Celcius.

Makes 8 large patties

Grilled Philly Cheesesteaks

"This grilled version of the classic Philly Cheesesteak has incredible "flame licked" flavour that would be non-existent in the traditional way of preparing it in a pan. I find the addition of mayonnaise is extremely important for not only adding richness, but also to help enhance the gooey drippy effect that a classic cheesesteak should have."

2 pounds (908g) rib-eye steaks
2 medium onions, sliced into 4 thick rounds each
2 red bell peppers, sliced into big pieces
Canola, vegetable or grape seed oil
Salt & pepper
1/2 cup butter
3 garlic cloves, finely minced
2 tbsp Worcestershire sauce
6 oval hoagie type buns
12 tbsp mayonnaise
360g provolone cheese slices

1. Preheat your BBQ over high heat. Oil the steaks with 3 to 4 tsp of the oil and then season liberally with salt & pepper. Toss the prepared onions and peppers with 1 tbsp of the oil.
2. Turn the heat on your BBQ to medium or medium/high and grill the steaks until your desired doneness, approximately 4 to 6 minutes per side for medium (depending on the temperature of the steaks and the power of your BBQ). Grill the onion and pepper slices at the same time just until they are somewhat charred and cooked through. Remove the steaks, onions and peppers and set aside.
3. Melt the butter, mix with the garlic and set aside.
4. Slice the peppers into thin strips and rough chop the onions. Toss these pepper and onion pieces together with the Worcestershire and season to taste with salt & pepper. Set aside.
5. Slice the steaks into very thin strips and toss with the reserved garlic butter and season to taste with salt & pepper. Set aside.
6. Prepare the buns by placing the cut side down on the grill and toasting them. Then spread 1 tbsp of mayonnaise on each the top and bottom toasted halves of the buns.

7. Top each open bun with equal amounts of the reserved steak slices, then equal amounts of the reserved onion/pepper mix, and then equal amounts of cheese slices. Place the open faced sandwiches on a baking sheet and broil in the oven until the cheese is thoroughly melted. Serve immediately.

Makes 6 large sandwiches

Quick Meat Marinade

1/4 cup full bodied red wine
1/4 cup olive oil
4 large garlic cloves, finely crushed or minced
1 tsp salt
1 tsp pepper
1 tsp dried oregano leaves
1 tsp dried basil leaves
1/2 tsp sambal oelek

1. Mix all ingredients together.
2. Pour over 2 to 4 steaks in a plastic bag. Press out the excess air, seal and let sit refrigerated for 2 to 24 hours. Tougher, less expensive cuts of beef will benefit more from the longer marinating time.
3. Remove steaks from marinade and grill to desired doneness.

Makes enough marinade for 2 to 4 steaks, depending on size of steaks

Guinness Shepherd's Pie

"A classic Irish pub favourite! Shepherd's Pie made with ground beef instead of the traditional ground lamb is actually called a Cottage Pie, but I kept the name Shepherd's Pie because it is more recognizable."

4 large russet potatoes, peeled and diced 1/2-inch
2 pounds (908g) lean ground beef
1 cup small diced onion
1 cup small diced carrot
1 cup small diced celery
6 garlic cloves, minced
1/4 cup flour
1 tbsp dried oregano
1 tbsp dried thyme
2 tsp salt
1 tsp pepper
1.5 tsp beef stock paste
1 – 156ml can tomato paste
1 – 440ml can Guinness beer
2 tbsp sugar
1 tbsp Worcestershire sauce
1 cup frozen peas
1/2 cup butter, cubed
2 tsp salt
1/2 tsp pepper
1 egg
1/4 cup whipping cream

1. Preheat the oven to 400 degrees.
2. Steam the potatoes for 20 minutes or until tender, set aside but keep warm over the water.
3. While the potatoes are steaming, brown the beef in a large pan over medium heat until all the liquid from the beef has evaporated, approximately 15 to 20 minutes.

4. To the beef, add the onion, carrot, celery, garlic, flour, oregano, thyme, 2 tsp salt, and 1 tsp pepper. Cook until softened a bit, approximately 5 to 7 minutes.
5. Stir in the beef stock paste and tomato paste until evenly distributed.
6. Stir in the Guinness, sugar, Worcestershire, and peas. Taste and re-season with salt and pepper if necessary. Remove from heat and let stand while mashing the potatoes.
7. Add the butter, 2 tsp salt, and 1/2 tsp pepper to the steamed potatoes and mash together until smooth.
8. In a small bowl thoroughly beat the egg and whipping cream together. Slowly add this to the mashed potatoes while incorporating to ensure that the egg doesn't become scrambled. Taste and re-season with salt and pepper if necessary.
9. Put the beef mixture into a 9 x 13 inch cake pan or casserole dish. Top evenly with the mashed potatoes and run a fork over the potatoes to make a design.
10. Bake for 30 minutes until the potato starts to brown. Let sit for at least 10 minutes before serving.

Makes approximately 8 to 12 portions

Pepper Steak Madagascar

2 top grade strip loin steaks
1.5 tbsp freshly cracked black peppercorns
Salt
1 tbsp oil
2/3 cup full bodied red wine
2 tbsp concord grape jelly (or other PREMIUM grape jelly)
1/3 - 1/2 cup whipping cream
1/2 cup beef stock
2 tbsp canned green Madagascar peppercorns, drained
1 tbsp butter
Fresh parsley, chopped – for garnish - optional

1. Season steaks with the crushed peppercorns and salt.
2. Heat a heavy pan over medium-high heat. Add oil and sear the steaks - approximately 2 minutes per side for rare (depending on thickness of steaks).
3. Remove the steaks from the pan, and cover them to keep warm.
4. Take the pan off the heat and carefully deglaze with the merlot.
5. Turn the heat to medium and replace the pan to the burner. Add the grape jelly and cook until the wine has reduced by half, and the jelly has melted into the wine.
6. Add the cream and beef stock. Turn the heat to medium-high and reduce until the sauce has almost thickened completely.
7. Add the green peppercorns.
8. Add the steaks back to the pan just to reheat and coat with the sauce.
9. Plate the steaks with the presentation side (the side with less fat) forward.
10. Reduce the sauce further until syrupy and stir in the butter. Taste and re-season if necessary.
11. Spoon the sauce over the steaks and down the front of the presentation sides. Garnish with fresh chopped parsley, if desired.

Makes 2 portions

Steaks with Merlot Reduction

"Red wine pan sauces are the quickest path to an incredible tasting steak. You've never had a steak fried in a pan taste so good... until now."

2 strip loin steaks
Salt & pepper
1 - 2 tsp grape seed oil or canola oil
½ (one half) tsp beef stock paste
½ (one half) cup Merlot or other full bodied red wine
¼ (one quarter) cup whipping cream
1 tsp sugar

1. Pre-heat a heavy bottomed pan over medium-high heat.
2. Season both sides of the steaks with salt and pepper.
3. When the pan is hot, add the oil and then the steaks. Cook for approximately two and one half minutes per side (for a total of 5 minutes) for rare to medium rare (depending on the temperature of the steaks, thickness of the steaks, and temperature of the pan).
4. Remove the steaks from the pan and let them rest.
5. Remove the pan from the heat temporarily and immediately add the beef stock paste and then deglaze with the Merlot.
6. Return the pan to the heat and stir in the whipping cream and sugar.
7. Boil the sauce, stirring constantly until syrupy – checking for consistency by occasionally removing the pan from the heat to let the boiling subside.
8. Pour the sauce immediately over the steaks and serve. If you are not pouring the sauce immediately over the steaks, then transfer the finished sauce to a small serving dish as the residual heat from the pan will continue to evaporate the sauce into an unusable paste.

Chef Dez note on this recipe - the term *"deglaze"* means to remove the browned bits (fond) in a hot pan by adding a liquid. This lifts the fond off of the pan and it becomes part of the sauce/finished dish.

Rack of Lamb with Blueberry Reduction

"A reduction sauce made from blueberries! It is important for the pan to be hot enough to sear the racks – this will add flavour to both the meat and the sauce."

2 racks of lamb approximately three-quarters of a pound each, frenched
2tbsp canola oil
Salt and freshly cracked pepper to taste
1/2 cup & a splash of full bodied red wine
2 cups blueberries
2.5 tsp white sugar
2 tsp beef stock paste
2-3 tbsp whipping cream

1. Oil the lamb racks with one tablespoon of the oil, and season them with salt and pepper.
2. Preheat oven to 450 degrees.
3. Heat a heavy bottomed pan over medium heat.
4. Add the other tablespoon of oil to the pan and sear the racks on both sides and ends. Approximately five minutes total.
5. Place the racks in a pan on a wire rack and roast in oven for fifteen minutes (approximately medium rare).
6. Deglaze the pan (remove the brown bits from the pan into the wine) with the splash of wine, scraping with a wooden spoon.
7. Add the other one half cup of wine, berries, sugar, and beef paste to the pan, and bring to a boil over medium high heat.
8. Reduce over the same temperature, while breaking up the berries with a spoon as they start to break down, approximately ten minutes. Mash the berries with a potato masher at this point.
9. Strain this sauce through a wire mesh strainer and return the sauce to the pan. Discard the pulp left in the strainer.
10. Add the cream and reduce the sauce until it is thick and syrupy.
11. Remove the sauce from the heat, and transfer the sauce to a different container and cover to prevent evaporation while waiting for the lamb to be cooked.

12. Remove the lamb racks from the oven and let rest for five minutes to allow meat to retain its juices. Plate by either leaving them whole or by cutting each chop individually.
13. Drizzle the sauce on and around the lamb.

Makes 2 - 6 servings

Southwestern Steak Diane

"A classic dish with a Southwestern twist! Increasing or decreasing the amount of chipotle peppers being used can control the spiciness of this dish."

4 strip loin steaks
2 tbsp canola oil
Salt & pepper
8 medium white mushrooms, sliced
2 tsp Worcestershire sauce
1 tbsp butter
1 – 2 chipotle peppers (canned), chopped
2 tbsp finely chopped onion
3 garlic cloves, finely minced
1 tbsp fresh lemon juice
1 tsp yellow mustard
2 tsp sugar
1/2 cup whipping cream
2 oz. Jack Daniels whiskey
Salt & fresh cracked pepper to taste
2 green onions, sliced for garnish

1. Oil the steaks with one tablespoon of the oil. Season them with salt & pepper.
2. Heat a heavy bottomed pan over medium to medium-high heat. Add the other tablespoon of oil and sear the steaks for approximately 3 to 4 minutes per side for medium-rare to medium steaks.
3. Remove the steaks from the pan and keep them covered to stay warm.
4. Turn the heat to medium and add the mushrooms and Worcestershire sauce and cook for approximately 1 minute.
5. Add the butter, chipotles, onion, and garlic – sauté until the mushrooms are completely cooked, approximately 2 – 3 minutes.
6. Add the lemon juice, mustard, sugar, and whipping cream to the pan. Stir to blend in, add the steaks back to the pan to reheat, and bring to a boil.
7. Once boiling, add the whiskey and ignite with a flame (be careful). Shake the pan until the flames reside and plate the steaks.

8. Return the pan to the burner and over medium-high heat, reduce the sauce until the desired syrupy consistency is reached. Season to taste with salt & pepper, and spoon the sauce over the steaks.
9. Garnish with green onion slices.

Makes 4 servings

Stewed Leg of Lamb

3 to 4 pound boneless leg of lamb
3 tbsp grape seed oil or canola oil
Salt & pepper
1/2 cup beef broth
1 small/medium carrot, diced small
1 stalk of celery, diced small
1 medium onion, diced small
8 cloves garlic, minced
1 tsp salt
1 – 796ml can diced tomatoes
1 cup red wine
3 to 4 tbsp chopped fresh rosemary
2 bay leaves
2 tbsp sugar
3 to 4 tbsp chopped fresh oregano
Salt & pepper to taste, if needed

1. Cut the lamb into 4 to 5 large pieces, coat with 2 tbsp of the oil and season with salt and pepper.
2. Preheat a large heavy bottomed pan over medium-high heat. When hot, add the other 1 tbsp of oil and immediately sear each piece of lamb on all sides until browned – only searing enough pieces at one time so that you don't crowd the pan. Remove and set aside.
3. Carefully deglaze the pan with the beef broth and then add the carrot, celery, onion, garlic, and salt. Cook for 2 to 3 minutes until soft.
4. Add the tomatoes, wine, rosemary, bay leaves, and the lamb to the pan. Bring to a boil and then cover and reduce the heat to low and simmer for 90 minutes, turning the lamb pieces over halfway through this cooking process.
5. After the 90 minute cooking time remove the lamb and set aside, tenting with foil to keep warm. Turn the heat to medium/high to high and boil to reduce the liquid until desired sauce consistency has been reached.
6. Remove from the heat. Remove and discard the bay leaves.

7. Stir in the sugar and fresh oregano. Taste and season with salt and pepper if desired. Cut the lamb into smaller desired chunks and stir back into the sauce. Serve immediately.

Makes approximately 6 to 8 portions

Maple & Bourbon Beef Short Ribs
"Recipe Created for Big Green Egg Canada and the Stihl Timbersports"

4 tbsp Sweet Smoked Paprika
2 tbsp Garlic Powder
4 tsp Salt
2 tsp Ground Black Pepper
2 tsp Dried Thyme
1/2 tsp ground cayenne pepper
6 large beef simmering short ribs (approx. 1.5kg total)
1/2 cup Maple Syrup
1/2 cup Bourbon Whiskey
1/4 cup Dark Brown Sugar
2 tbsp Prepared Seed Mustard or your Favorite Mustard

1. Prepare your Big Green Egg for indirect cooking with the ConvEGGtor with Big Green Egg Oak & Hickory Charcoal and steady temperature to 225 degrees Fahrenheit. If desired additional smoking chips can be included in with the charcoal.
2. Mix together the paprika, garlic powder, salt, pepper, thyme, and cayenne.
3. Liberally coat all surfaces of the ribs with this spice mixture.
4. Place the ribs on the cooking grid. Lower the lid and cook at 225 degrees for 6 hours, or until the internal temperature of the ribs reach 190 degrees Fahrenheit.
5. While the ribs are cooking, combine the maple syrup, bourbon, brown sugar, and mustard in a small pot. Bring to a boil over medium heat and cook this mixture until only just under 1 cup of this mixture remains. Reducing the heat to medium-low in the process to prevent the mixture from boiling over. Stirring occasionally. Remove from the heat and let cool in the pot at room temperature.
6. Remove the ribs from the cooking grid and place them in a small cooler for 1 hour. This process will not only continue to raise the temperature of the ribs, but also help to make them more tender. The smaller the cooler the better (not too much excess space around the ribs).

7. Plate the ribs and drizzle the reduced maple and bourbon sauce over them. Serve immediately.

Makes 6 large ribs

PORK

Dublin Coddle

Apricot Pecan Pork Chops

Cinnamon Roasted Pork Tenderloin with Applesauce

Drunken Pig

Fiery Asian Grilled Pork Chops

Peach & Thyme Pork Chops

Grandma G's BBQ Ribs

Mediterranean Stuffed Pork Loin

Mexican Chipotle Papaya Pork

Pork Medallions in Single Malt Pan Sauce

Spicy "Peach & Heat" Pork on Rice

Dublin Coddle

"Rustic Irish cooking at its best! This classic casserole is made up of potatoes and sausages and baked to perfection with a combination of chicken broth, cream and Guinness beer."

12 large pork, beef or Italian sausages
4 extra-large russet potatoes, peeled and sliced very thin
8 bacon strips, sliced into 1/4 inch pieces
4 medium onions, chopped
6 cloves of garlic, finely chopped
1 tbsp salt
1 tsp sugar
1 tsp dried sage
Pepper
1/2 cup chicken broth
1/2 cup whipping cream
1/2 cup Guinness beer
Finely chopped parsley, for garnish

1. Heat large non-stick pan over medium heat. Add the sausages and cook until browned on all sides, approximately 8 to 12 minutes. Set sausages aside and discard the fat from the pan.
2. While the sausages are cooking, preheat oven to 350 degrees, and arrange potato slices into a large deep casserole dish, or preferably a large cast iron pot.
3. Return the pan to the stove and increase the heat to medium-high. Add the bacon, onions, garlic, salt, sugar, sage and season with pepper. Cook until the onions are soft and slightly browned, approximately 5 to 10 minutes.
4. Spread this onion/bacon mixture evenly over the potato slices.
5. Pour the broth, cream and beer over the entire dish.
6. Place the sausages on top. Cover and cook for 1 hour in the preheated oven.
7. Sprinkle with the chopped parsley and serve "family style", by dishing it out at the table.

Serves 6 to 8 people.

Apricot Pecan Pork Chops

4 cups cold water
1/4 cup salt
1/4 cup brown sugar (not golden sugar)
4 – one-inch thick bone-in pork chops
100g pecan halves, approximately 3/4 cup
1 tbsp grape seed oil or canola oil
Pepper
1/2 cup white wine
6 garlic cloves, minced
250g dried apricots (approximately 1.75 cups), cut into quarters
1.5 cups chicken broth
1 tbsp brown sugar (not golden sugar)
1 to 2 tsp sambal oelek
1 tbsp apple cider vinegar
1/4 cup whipping cream

1. Add the water, salt and the quarter cup brown sugar to a large bowl and whisk vigorously until the salt and sugar have dissolved. Place the pork chops in a large freezer bag and pour this brine over them. Squeeze out as much air as possible when closing the bag and then place the bag of brine/chops back into the bowl and refrigerate for 1 to 2 hours.
2. While the chops are brining, toast the pecans and set aside. The pecans can be easily toasted in a small dry pan over medium heat, while tossing occasionally, for approximately 5 to 10 minutes. Watch them carefully as they can burn easily due to their high fat content.
3. Preheat the oven to 425 degrees Fahrenheit. Remove the chops from the brine and pat them dry to remove any excess moisture. Preheat a large heavy bottomed pan over medium-high heat. Coat the chops with the oil and season them with pepper.
4. Once the pan is hot, sear the chops on both sides for approximately 3 to 4 minutes per side. Then transfer the chops to a broiler pan and bake in the oven for approximately 8 to 10 minutes. Remove and let them rest for at least 5 minutes.

5. When the chops are put into the oven, drain any excess fat off the pan. Turn down the stove to medium heat and place the pan back on the heat – immediately add the white wine carefully to the pan to deglaze (scrape the browned bits off the bottom with a wooden spoon). Add the garlic, apricots, chicken broth, 1 tbsp brown sugar, and sambal oelek. Stir to combine and cook for approximately 8 to 10 minutes, stirring occasionally, until it has become syrupy.
6. Stir in the vinegar and whipping cream, and reduce again until syrupy, approximately 2 to 3 minutes more. Serve over the resting chops and garnish with the reserved toasted pecans.

Makes 4 servings

Cinnamon Roasted Pork Tenderloin with Applesauce

"The tenderloin is brined in salt water to help keep it juicy and flavourful"

4 cups cold water
1/4 cup table salt
1 lb pork tenderloin
1 tbsp cinnamon
1 tsp paprika
1/2 tsp salt
1/4 tsp pepper
1/4 tsp ground cumin
1 tbsp olive oil
1 tsp liquid honey
Mint leaves (for garnish), optional

Applesauce
1/2 cup white wine
1 tsp lemon juice
2 large apples, peeled, cored, & sliced thin
1 tbsp white sugar
1/4 tsp allspice
Pinch of salt

1. Dissolve the 1/4 cup table salt in the 4 cups of water. Add the tenderloin, and brine for one hour in the refrigerator.
2. Remove the tenderloin and pat dry. Mix the next seven ingredients in a small bowl to make a wet rub. Apply this rub to all areas of the tenderloin, and let sit in the refrigerator for 1/2 hour to 12 hours.
3. Preheat the oven to 400 degrees. Roast the tenderloin in the oven for 20 –25 minutes. Let sit for 5 – 10 minutes before slicing. Serve with the applesauce, and garnish with a mint leaf sprig.

Applesauce

1. Add all the ingredients for the applesauce to a non-reactive (stainless steel) pot.

2. Bring to a boil over medium-high heat while breaking up the apples with a wooden spoon.
3. Lower the heat to medium-low and simmer for 20 minutes.
4. Mash the apples until desired consistency is reached, and hold covered off the heat until needed.

Makes 2 - 4 servings

Drunken Pig

"Lots of pork with lots of wine! Perfect when served with my recipe for Garlic Mashed Potatoes."

Salt & pepper
1.5 kg pork butt roast
2 tbsp canola or grape seed oil
1 medium onion, diced small
6 – 8 garlic cloves, minced
1.5 (one and one half) cups and a splash of full bodied red wine
2 sprigs fresh rosemary (plus more for garnish)
1 bay leaf
2 tbsp tomato paste
2 tsp white sugar
Salt & fresh cracked pepper to taste, if desired
1-2 tsp butter (optional)

1. Remove the string from roast, and cut into 3 or 4 equal pieces.
2. Lightly season roast pieces with salt and pepper.
3. Heat a heavy bottomed pan over medium-high heat.
4. Add oil to pan and brown the pork on all sides, in two batches if using a smaller pan.
5. Remove the pork and set aside.
6. Cool down the pan a bit, and sauté the onion and garlic over medium heat for about 2 minutes until softened a bit.
7. Deglaze the pan with a splash of wine.
8. Add the pork, rosemary, bay leaf, and 1-½ cups of wine to the pan; bring to a boil over high heat.
9. Turn down to simmer; cover and cook over med-low heat for 2 hours. *Half way through the cooking time, flip the pork pieces over.
10. Remove the pork and set aside covered with foil to keep warm. Discard the Bay leaf and the rosemary sprigs.
11. Increase the heat to high, add the tomato paste and the sugar, and reduce the liquid for about 10-15 minutes until syrupy.
12. Taste and adjust seasonings if needed.

13. Finish the sauce by removing from heat and stirring in butter until just melted (optional).
14. Cut the pork into bite-sized pieces or slices.
15. Serve immediately; plate a mound of "Garlic Mashed Potatoes" in the center with a few pork pieces on top. Drizzle a couple tablespoons of sauce over the pork and on the plate around the mashed potatoes.
16. Garnish with freshly chopped parsley and a sprig of fresh rosemary.

Serves 6 to 8 people with "Garlic Mashed Potatoes"

Fiery Asian Grilled Pork Chops

"By cooking the residual marinade into a reduction glaze to finish the chops, they become so delectably delicious and scream with flavor. Splenda brand sweetener is used instead of sugar, because sugar will burn."

1/4 cup Splenda granulated sweetener
1/4 cup soy sauce
6 – 8 garlic cloves, crushed
1 tbsp fresh minced ginger
1 tbsp sambal oelek (crushed chili paste/liquid)
1 tsp sesame oil
4 - 6   boneless pork loin center chops, approx. 700g total
1 – 2 green onions, sliced diagonally, for garnish
White and/or black sesame seeds, for garnish

1. Combine Splenda, soy sauce, garlic, ginger, sambal oelek, and sesame oil. Add the pork chops and toss thoroughly. Cover or put in a sealed freezer bag and marinate in the refrigerator for 1 to 6 hours, tossing occasionally.
2. Preheat bar-be-que grill with a high flame. Remove chops from the marinade and put the residual marinade in a small pot.
3. Cook the pork chops on the grill over a medium flame until cooked through, approximately 4 to 7 minutes per side depending on the thickness of the chops and temperature of the grill.
4. Boil the residual marinade at a full boil for approximately 1 to 2 minutes.
5. Brush the cooked marinade onto the pork chops once they have been flipped on the grill.
6. Serve each pork chop garnished with a few green onion slices and a sprinkle of sesame seeds.

Makes 4 to 6 portions

Peach and Thyme Pork Chops

"The amount of sugar you use will depend on the sweetness of your peaches — start with one tablespoon and then add the other tablespoon at the end if needed"

6 pork loin center chops, boneless
1 tbsp canola oil
Salt & pepper
1/2 cup white wine
1/2 cup chicken broth
5 to 6 peaches, peeled, pitted, and sliced
3 cloves of garlic, minced
2 tbsp fresh thyme leaves
1 to 2 tbsp sugar

1. Heat a large heavy bottomed pan over medium-high heat.
2. Coat the chops with oil and season both sides with salt & pepper. Sear the chops on both sides, approximately 3 to 4 minutes total.
3. Add the wine, broth, peaches, garlic, thyme and sugar to the pan and stir slightly to combine and bring to a boil.
4. Cover, turn the heat down to medium-low, and cook for 8 minutes.
5. Remove the lid, turn the chops over, and cook with no lid for another 7 minutes.
6. Remove the chops from the pan and set them aside. Increase the heat to medium-high and reduce the sauce until syrupy. Serve immediately.

Makes 6 portions

Grandma G's BBQ Ribs

"When my Mom was a child, they raised pigs on a farm, and my Grandma would make ribs quite often with a homemade BBQ sauce very similar to this."

2-3 racks of pork ribs
Salt & Pepper for seasoning
1/2 cup ketchup
1/4 cup HP Sauce
1/4 cup brown sugar
2 tbsp white vinegar
1 tbsp lemon juice
1/2 tsp pepper
1/2 tsp salt
1/2 tsp cinnamon
Dash of cloves
2 garlic cloves, crushed
2 tsp vegetable oil (however, if you want to keep this recipe closer to the original used by my Grandma, use 2 tbsp melted butter as they didn't have vegetable oil on the farm)

1. Preheat the oven to 450 degrees.
2. Season both sides of the ribs with salt and pepper and place them on a cookie sheet(s).
3. Sear the ribs in the oven for 30 minutes. While ribs are searing, mix all the remaining ingredients to create the BBQ sauce.
4. Remove the ribs from the oven and lower the oven temperature to 300 degrees.
5. Brush the ribs on both sides with the BBQ sauce. Pour 1/2 cup water onto the cookie sheet and put the ribs back onto the cookie sheet. Cover the sheet with enough aluminum foil to tightly seal over the edges of the cookie sheet (this will hold in the steam that will slowly cook the ribs).
6. Place inside the oven and bake at 300 degrees for 1-1/2 hours.
7. Lower the oven temperature to 250 degrees and bake for another 1-1/2 hours. It is very important to not open up the sealed tray of ribs.
8. Remove the tray of ribs and turn the oven to "broil".

9. ALL OF THE FOLLOWING STEPS MUST BE DONE CAREFULLY, AS THE RIBS ARE NOW SO TENDER THAT THEY WILL FALL OFF THE BONES
10. Pierce the aluminum foil in the corner and gently pour out the water.
11. Remove and discard the aluminum foil. Gently brush the top of the ribs liberally with the sauce.
12. Broil the ribs on the tray in the oven for a few minutes until the sauce on the top has caramelized.
13. Gently remove the ribs off the tray and transfer onto a serving platter by sliding a couple of long utensils (tongs, for example) underneath each rack in order to not disturb the shape of the racks.

Makes 4 – 6 servings

Mediterranean Stuffed Pork Loin Roast

400g Italian sausage
1/2 cup chopped & drained sundried tomatoes
1/3 cup grated Parmesan cheese
6 garlic cloves, crushed
1 egg
2 tsp fennel seeds
1 tsp dried oregano
1 tsp freshly ground pepper
1/2 tsp dried basil
1/4 tsp salt
1 kg boneless pork loin roast
1/3 cup finely crumbled feta cheese
fresh spinach leaves
cotton butcher's cord
salt & pepper
2 tbsp vegetable oil

1. Preheat oven to 350 degrees.
2. Squeeze sausage from casings into a medium sized mixing bowl.
3. Add the tomatoes, parmesan, garlic, egg, fennel, oregano, pepper, basil, and salt to the sausage, and mix together.
4. To flatten the roast for stuffing: With a large knife, cut the bottom 1/3 of the roast lengthwise without cutting through the opposite side. Continue to cut the remaining 2/3 of the roast in half lengthwise. The result should be one long, thin rectangle of pork.
5. Spread the sausage mixture evenly across the pork, leaving a 1/2 inch border around the edge.
6. Press the crumbled feta cheese evenly into the sausage mixture.
7. Lay a single layer of spinach leaves over the entire surface of the sausage and cheese.
8. Gently roll up the roast; back in the same direction that it was cut to its original shape, making sure that it is not too tight. Tie the roast firmly with loops of the butcher's cord every ½ to 1 inch all the way across

the roast. Finish tying with one more loop lengthwise to fully secure the roast/stuffing.

9. Season the outside of the roast liberally with salt and pepper.
10. Heat a large heavy bottomed pan over medium-high heat. Add the vegetable oil and sear the roast on all sides until completely browned.
11. Place the roast on a rack in a shallow baking pan, insert a meat thermometer, and bake until the internal temperature reaches 160 degrees Fahrenheit, approximately 2 hours.
12. Remove from the oven and let it rest for 15 minutes before carving and serving.

Makes 6 – 8 servings

Mexican Chipotle Papaya Pork

"The chunks of sweet papaya adds a wonderful contrast to the smoky heat of the chipotle peppers"

2 pork tenderloins, approximately 600g total
4 tbsp grape seed oil, or canola oil
Salt & Pepper
1 medium onion, chopped
6 garlic cloves, chopped
1 tbsp canned green chillies
1 – 2 canned chipotle peppers
2 tsp Mexican chilli powder
1 tsp salt
1/4 cup chicken broth
1 medium/large red bell pepper, diced half inch
1 tbsp sugar
1 cup whipping cream
1/4 cup finely chopped cilantro
Juice of 1/2 lime
1/2 Caribbean Red Papaya, cubed large, (approximately 2 cups)
Cooked rice

1. Cube the tenderloins by cutting them in half lengthwise, and then cut into one half inch pieces. Toss the pork chunks with 2 tbsp of the oil and season with some salt and pepper.
2. Heat a large pan over medium high heat. Once hot, add the other 2 tbsp of the oil and then cook the pork until browned and just cooked through, stirring occasionally, approximately 5 to 6 minutes. Remove the pork with a slotted spoon and set aside.
3. Turn the heat to medium. Add the onion, garlic, green chillies, chipotle peppers, chilli powder, and salt. Stir together and cook, stirring occasionally for approximately 2 to 3 minutes.
4. Add the chicken broth and stir to lift off all the flavours from the pan.
5. Stir in the reserved pork (and any pork juices), red pepper, and the sugar.

6. Stir in the cream and reduce over medium high heat until thickened, approximately 2 to 3 minutes.
7. Remove from the heat and stir in the cilantro and lime juice. Season to taste with more salt and pepper if desired.
8. Stir in the papaya chunks and serve immediately with cooked rice.

Makes approximately 4 to 6 portions

Pork Medallions in Single Malt Pan Sauce

"Live like the Scots — Scotch is not just for drinking, it's for cooking too!"

1 - 500g pork tenderloin
2 tsp canola oil
Salt & pepper
1/2 cup chicken broth
1/4 cup peaty single malt scotch
Juice of 1/2 lemon
1 tbsp liquid honey
1/4 cup whipping cream

1. Cut the tenderloin into 12 equal sized medallions, approximately one half inch to three quarter inch thickness. Toss with the oil and season both sides with salt and pepper.
2. Heat a heavy bottomed pan over medium high heat.
3. When the pan is hot add the medallions and sear them for approximately 2 to 3 minutes on each side.
4. Add the chicken stock to the pan to deglaze (stir briefly to remove the browned bits off the pan into the sauce).
5. Add the Scotch carefully and ignite with a long match. Flambé until the flames subside.
6. Add the lemon juice, honey and cream. Continue to boil until syrupy and desired sauce consistency. Remove from heat, lightly season to taste with salt and pepper, and serve immediately.

Makes 4 portions (3 medallions each)

Spicy 'Peach & Heat' Pork on Rice

680g (1.5 pounds) pork tenderloins
Salt & pepper
4 tbsp grape seed oil or canola oil
1.5 cups large diced onion
1 cup sliced celery, cut on an angle
1 cup thin sliced carrot, cut on an angle
6 garlic cloves, finely chopped
1 tsp salt
1 to 2 tbsp sambal oelek
1 cup peach jam
2 – 398ml cans sliced peaches in juice, drained, peaches and 1 cup of juice reserved
1 cup chicken broth
3 tbsp cornstarch, dissolved in a few tbsp of the chicken broth
Cooked rice
Angle cut sliced green onions, for garnish

1. Cut the pork tenderloins in half lengthwise, and then cut into approximately half-inch chunks. Toss the pork chunks with salt & pepper and 2 tbsp of the oil.
2. Heat a wok over medium-high heat and once hot, add the other 2 tbsp of oil to the wok. Fry the pork in small batches until browned, removing with a slotted spoon and setting aside each batch.
3. Add the onion, celery, carrot, garlic and the 1 tsp salt to the wok. Stir fry for 1 minute.
4. Add the reserved pork (and any remaining juices from the pork) and the sambal oelek. Stir fry for 2 to 3 minutes more.
5. Stir in the peach jam. Add the 1 cup of reserved juice, chicken broth, and the dissolved cornstarch mixture. Heat over high heat until boiling and sauce has thickened.
6. Remove from the heat, stir in the reserved peach slices and serve immediately on cooked rice. Garnish with the green onion.

Makes approximately 4 to 6 full portions

RECIPE NOTES

POULTRY

Greek Rubbed Chicken

Chicken Provencale

Coq au Vin

Grilled Blueberry Brie Chicken Sandwich

Low Salt Chicken & Turkey Rub

Hold My Chipotle Beer Pasta

Pan Roasted Duck Breast with Red Wine Reduction

Indian Butter Chicken

Mexican Mole Sauce for Chicken

Patricia's Mediterranean Chicken

Greek Rubbed Chicken

4 tsp dried oregano leaves
4 tsp granulated onion
4 tsp granulated garlic
4 tsp dried parsley
4 tsp dried rosemary
4 tsp sugar
2 tsp cornstarch
2 tsp salt
2 tsp ground pepper
Zest from 2 lemons, finely grated or chopped
6 to 8 bone-in pieces of chicken
Olive oil
Juice from 1 small lemon

1. Preheat the oven to 400 degrees Fahrenheit.
2. In a small bowl combine the oregano, onion, garlic, parsley, rosemary, sugar, salt, pepper, cornstarch, and lemon zest to form a dry rub. Set aside.
3. Rub the chicken pieces on both sides with some olive oil. Dredge the chicken pieces in the dry rub from step number 2, making sure it is applied to all areas and crevices of the chicken.
4. Place the chicken, skin side up, on a rack on a baking pan. Bake in the oven for approximately 40 minutes until an instant read thermometer, in the thickest parts of the pieces, reads 160 degrees Fahrenheit.
5. Remove from the oven and immediately squeeze the half lemon over the chicken.

Makes 6 to 8 portions

Chicken Provençale

"Soaking the chicken breasts in the salt-water brine helps to keep them moist and flavourful"

6 tbsp table salt
6 cups water
4 boneless, skinless chicken breasts
Flour for dredging
3 tbsp olive oil
1 medium shallot, minced
6 – 8 garlic cloves, minced
1 anchovy or 1 tsp anchovy paste
2 tsp dried oregano
1 – 796ml can of diced tomatoes, drained
1 cup white wine
2 tsp white sugar
2 tbsp tomato paste
10 calamata olives, pitted and minced
Fresh oregano leaves, chopped for garnish

1. Dissolve the salt in 6 cups cold water. Submerse the chicken breasts in this salt-water brine for at least 1 hour in the refrigerator.
2. Take chicken out of the brine and pat dry with paper towels. Discard brine. Dredge chicken in flour to lightly coat.
3. Heat a heavy bottomed pan over medium-high heat. Add 2 tbsp of the olive oil and brown the chicken on both sides, approximately 3 minutes per side. Do not crowd the pan – if the pan is too crowded, the chicken will steam in their juices rather than brown. Once browned, remove chicken from pan and set aside.
4. Cool down the pan a bit by adding half of the tomatoes and turn down the heat to medium.
5. Add the third tbsp of olive oil, shallot, garlic, anchovy, and oregano and sauté for about 2 minutes until shallot and garlic are softened.
6. Add the rest of the tomatoes, wine, and the chicken breasts. Turn heat to high and bring to a boil.

7. Reduce the heat to simmer, cover and cook over med-low heat for 20 minutes.
8. Remove the chicken and set aside covered with foil to keep warm.
9. Increase heat to high, add the tomato paste and the sugar. Reduce the liquid by boiling for approximately 5 minutes until it has reached desired consistency, stirring occasionally.
10. Remove the sauce from the heat and stir in the olives. Serve immediately; plate one chicken breast per plate, and spoon sauce over it, and garnish with fresh oregano leaves. Great on its own or serve on rice or pasta

Makes 4 portions

Coq au Vin

"Don't be intimidated by the fancy French name. It is simply pronounced, "coke oh van" and loosely translated is "chicken in wine", or more precisely "rooster in wine"."

1/3 cup flour, seasoned with salt & pepper
4 chicken thighs
3 thick bacon slices, cut into 1/4 inch pieces
10 medium to large mushrooms, quartered
12 pearl onions, peeled and left whole
2-3 garlic cloves, crushed
1 tsp dried thyme leaves
1 cup and a splash of red wine
2 bay leaves
salt & fresh cracked pepper, to taste
1-2 tsp butter (optional)
fresh chopped parsley and fresh thyme for garnish (optional)

1. Heat heavy bottomed pan over medium heat.
2. Dredge chicken in the seasoned flour.
3. Add the bacon to the pan and render it until almost crisp; remove with a slotted spoon and set aside.
4. Turn the heat to medium-high and brown the chicken pieces in the bacon fat on both sides; approximately 6 minutes total - Remove the chicken and set aside with the bacon pieces.
5. Lower heat to medium and add the mushrooms, onions, garlic and thyme; sauté for approximately 2-3 minutes until softened a bit. Then deglaze the pan (loosen the browned bits cooked on the pan) with a splash of Pinot Noir and a wooden spoon.
6. Add the bacon, chicken, 1 cup Pinot Noir, and bay leaves; bring to a boil over medium-high heat. Once boiling, turn down to simmer; cover and cook for 30-35 minutes until the chicken is cooked through.
7. Remove the chicken thighs, onions, mushrooms, and bacon with a slotted spoon and set aside covered with foil to keep warm. Discard the Bay leaves.

8. Increase the heat to medium-high and reduce the liquid by about half, approximately 5 minutes. Taste and adjust the seasonings with salt and fresh cracked pepper after it has reduced.
9. Finish the sauce by removing the pan from the heat and stirring in the butter until just melted (optional).
10. Serve immediately: plate each chicken thigh with 3 onions, 10 mushroom quarters, a few bacon pieces, and drizzle a couple tablespoons of sauce over and around chicken.
11. If desired, garnish with fresh chopped parsley, and a sprig of fresh thyme.

Makes 4 portions

Grilled Blueberry Brie Chicken Sandwich

"The balance between the sweet blueberries and blueberry syrup with the pungent creaminess of the garlic cream cheese is incredible when paired with the grilled chicken and melted brie cheese. I know that the inclusion of blueberries and syrup in a chicken sandwich sounds odd, but you need to try this — your taste buds will thank you!"

125g spreadable cream cheese
1 large garlic clove, finely crushed or minced
1/4 tsp salt
4 chicken breast halves, cut butterflied to make them thinner
3 tbsp olive oil
Salt & pepper
1 – 454g flat ciabatta bread loaf
100g brie cheese, sliced thin
4 tbsp blueberry syrup
1 1/3 (one and one third) cups fresh blueberries (approximately)

1. Preheat grill over high heat.
2. Place the 125g cream cheese in a small mixing bowl and combine with the garlic and 1/4 teaspoon of salt.
3. Oil the chicken with 1 tbsp of the olive oil and season with salt and pepper.
4. Grill the chicken over medium heat/flame until cooked through, flipping only once, approximately 2 to 4 minutes per side depending on the thickness and temperature of the chicken.
5. Cut the ciabatta loaf into four equal pieces and then cut each of the four pieces in half horizontally to create a sandwich top and bottom with each one. Brush the other 2 tbsp of olive oil over the cut sides of the bread and grill cut/oiled side down until lightly toasted.
6. When the chicken is almost cooked, distribute the brie slices evenly over the chicken and close the lid on the BBQ to melt the cheese, approximately 1 to 2 minutes. ~ Or ~ alternatively once the chicken is cooked distribute the brie slices evenly over the chicken and broil in the oven until cheese is melted.
7. Assemble each of the four sandwiches as follows: On the bottom half of each sandwich, drizzle 1 tbsp blueberry syrup and place the

chicken/brie on top of it. On the top half of each sandwich spread 1/4 of the garlic cream cheese mixture and 1/3 (one third) cup of fresh blueberries gently pressed into the surface of the garlic cream cheese.

8. Serve open faced to display the blueberries and the melted brie on the chicken.

Makes 4 sandwiches

Low Salt Chicken & Turkey Rub

"Use this low salt rub when you already have enough salt content from brining chicken & turkey"

6 bay leaves
5 tbsp black peppercorns
4 tbsp garlic powder
4 tbsp ground dry mustard
2 tbsp smoked paprika
2 tbsp salt
2 tbsp brown sugar
2 tbsp chilli powder
2 tsp ground cinnamon

Grind the bay leaves and the peppercorns together in a spice grinder. Mix everything together.

Hold My Chipotle Beer Pasta

"I wrote this recipe for country Artist Aaron Pritchett"

3 tbsp canola oil
680g (1.5 pounds) chicken breast filets, cut into bite-sized pieces
Salt & pepper
1 medium onion, finely diced
6 to 8 garlic cloves, minced
2.5 (two and one half) tsp salt
1/2 tsp pepper
2 – 796ml (28 fl oz.) cans diced tomatoes, drained
156ml (5.5 fl oz.) can tomato paste
2 tbsp white sugar
1 tbsp dried oregano leaves
1 tbsp dried thyme leaves
2 chipotle peppers (canned), minced
440ml can Guinness beer, or other dark stout
375g-package whole-wheat linguine pasta
Fresh parsley, chopped fine, for garnish

1. Heat a heavy-bottomed pan over medium-high heat.
2. Add the canola oil and the chicken pieces and season lightly with salt & pepper. Stir occasionally until browned and cooked through.
3. Remove chicken with a slotted spoon.
4. Reduce the heat to medium – add the onions, then the garlic and the salt & pepper. Cook 2 to 3 minutes until soft, stirring occasionally.
5. Add the drained tomatoes, tomato paste, sugar, oregano, thyme, and chipotle peppers. Stir to combine.
6. Add the beer. Increase the heat to medium-high and bring to a boil.
7. Reduce the heat and simmer uncovered until the sauce reaches desired consistency, approximately 5 minutes.
8. While sauce is reducing, cook pasta according to package instructions.
9. Stir chicken pieces into the sauce. Toss in the cooked pasta and serve immediately, garnished with chopped parsley.

Makes 4 to 6 portions

Pan Roasted Duck Breast with Red Wine Reduction

2 boneless duck breasts, skin on
Salt and pepper
1/2 tsp beef stock paste
1/2 to 3/4 cup full bodied red wine
1/2 tsp sugar
2 - 3 tbsp heavy cream (whipping cream)

1. Score the skin (not the flesh underneath) of the duck breasts many times in two diagonal directions to create half-inch diamond shapes in the skin. Season both sides of the duck breasts with salt and pepper.
2. Preheat the oven to 400 degrees F.
3. Place the seasoned, scored duck breasts, skin side down, in a cold oven-proof pan big enough to ensure there is space between the two breasts. Place the pan over medium heat and do not disturb the duck breasts except to spoon off the rendered fat from the skin. They will release from the pan once the skin has crisped in approximately 10 to 13 minutes. Keep spooning off the rendered fat into a separate dish during this process.
4. Once the skin side has crisped, turn the heat to medium high and brown the flesh side of the duck breasts for approximately 1 minute.
5. Place the pan in the preheated oven and cook until medium-rare (135-140 degrees F internal temperature on the thickest part of the breast), approximately 7 to 8 minutes.
6. Remove the breasts and side aside to rest for 8 to 10 minutes. Remove the residual fat from the pan.
7. Let the pan cool a bit before adding the beef stock paste and then slowly adding the red wine to deglaze. Place the pan over medium-high heat (be careful of the hot handle from the oven) and add the sugar and cream. Stir constantly while reducing the sauce into a syrupy consistency and then transfer the sauce immediately to a separate container to prevent further evaporation from the hot pan.
8. Serve the hot wine reduction with the rested duck breasts immediately.

Makes 2 portions

Indian Butter Chicken

2 cups canned diced tomatoes, not drained
1 – 156ml can tomato paste
2/3 cup plain yogurt (full fat)
1/2 cup ground almonds
4 garlic cloves, crushed
4 tbsp dark brown sugar
3 tsp sambal oelek
3 tsp chili powder
2 tsp garam masala
2 tsp finely minced fresh ginger
1.5 tsp salt
1/2 tsp ground cloves
1/2 tsp ground cinnamon
1 kg boneless, skinless chicken thighs
6 green cardamom pods
2 whole bay leaves
1/4 cup + 2 tbsp butter
1 tbsp canola oil
2 medium onions, thinly sliced
salt & pepper
1/2 cup whipping cream
1 tbsp cornstarch
4 tbsp chopped fresh cilantro
cooked basmati rice

1. In a large mixing bowl, combine together the tomatoes, tomato paste, yogurt, almonds, garlic, brown sugar, sambal oelek, chili powder, garam masala, ginger, salt, cloves, and cinnamon.
2. Cut the chicken into bite-sized pieces and stir in to the mixture.
3. Gently pinch the cardamom pods to open them up a bit and add them whole along with the bay leaves to the chicken mixture.
4. Let marinate in the refrigerator for 1 to 4 hours.

5. In a heavy bottomed pot or large deep skillet, melt the butter and oil together over medium-high heat. Add the onions, season with salt & pepper, and sauté until soft, approximately 3 minutes.
6. Add the chicken & marinade mixture and continue to cook over medium-high heat until the chicken is cooked through, approximately 7 – 10 minutes, stirring occasionally.
7. Remove the whole bay leaves and cardamom pods.
8. Mix the whipping cream and the cornstarch together, and pour into the boiling chicken mixture while stirring. Bring the mixture to a boil once again to ensure the full thickening power of the cornstarch.
9. Stir in 2 tbsp of the cilantro and serve over rice, garnishing with the remaining cilantro.

Makes 4 to 6 servings

Mexican Mole Sauce for Chicken
"Big bold flavour with smoky heat, finished with unsweetened chocolate"

1 tbsp cumin seed
2 inch stick of cinnamon
2 dry bay leaves
1 tbsp dry oregano leaves
2 tbsp canola oil
1/3 cup peanuts
1/3 cup slivered almonds
1/3 cup raisins
1 medium onion, chopped
6 garlic cloves, chopped
2 tsp salt
1/2 tsp pepper
2 to 3 canned chipotle peppers
1 – 796ml can diced tomatoes, drained well
2oz. unsweetened chocolate, chopped
2 cups chicken broth
1/4 cup dark brown sugar
Juice of 1 lime
Cooked chicken & cooked rice
Sour cream & chopped fresh cilantro, optional

1. Heat cumin seeds and cinnamon stick in a large pan over medium heat until the seeds start to smoke and become fragrant, approximately 3 to 4 minutes. Transfer to a spice grinder with the bay leaves and oregano and process until fully ground. Set aside.
2. Return the pan to the heat until hot. Add the oil and fry the peanuts and almonds until coloured, approximately 1 to 2 minutes. BE CAREFUL NOT TO BURN THEM. Remove with a slotted spoon and set aside.
3. Return the oiled pan to the heat, add the raisins and fry them for approximately 30 seconds until they are plump. BE CAREFUL NOT TO BURN THEM. Remove with a slotted spoon and set aside with the nuts.

4. Return the pan to the heat. Add the onion, garlic, salt and pepper. Cook until the onion just starts to caramelize, approximately 1 to 2 minutes. Then add the chipotle peppers and the drained tomatoes and cook for 2 minutes more.
5. Add all of the above (ground spices, peanuts, almonds, raisins, onion, garlic, chipotles, and tomatoes) to a blender or food processor. Add 1 cup of the chicken broth and process until smooth. *Optional – pass through a strainer after pureeing for a completely smooth consistency.
6. Add this pureed sauce back to the pan over medium heat. Add the chocolate, the other cup of chicken broth, and the brown sugar. Heat until the chocolate has melted and the sauce is hot.
7. Remove the pan from the heat and stir in the lime juice. Season to taste with salt and pepper and serve over cooked chicken and rice. Top each portion with a dollop of sour cream and a sprinkle of chopped cilantro, optional.

Makes 5 cups of sauce

Patricia's Mediterranean Chicken

"I wrote this recipe for country artist Patricia Conroy. Goat cheese covered grilled chicken topped with a sundried tomato & artichoke sauce infused with garlic, white wine, fresh lemon juice and basil. Very rich and very delicious."

6 boneless, skinless chicken breast halves
Olive oil
Salt & pepper
2 tbsp butter
3 to 4 garlic cloves, minced
2 tbsp minced onion
1/2 cup dry white wine
1/4 cup fresh lemon juice (approx. 2 lemons or less), zest reserved
1 cup chopped oil packed sundried tomatoes, drained
1 – 398ml/14 oz. can artichoke hearts, drained and quartered
1/4 cup whipping cream
2 tsp sugar
1/2 tsp salt
1/2 tsp pepper
2/3 cup cold butter, cut in small pieces
1/4 cup chopped fresh basil
227g soft unripened goat cheese

1. Brush the chicken breasts with olive oil and season with salt and pepper. Grill over a medium flame for approximately 15 to 20 minutes until cooked through.
2. While chicken is cooking prepare the sauce. Melt the 2 tbsp butter in a pan over medium heat. Add the garlic and onion and sauté until soft, approximately 2 to 3 minutes.
3. Stir in the wine and lemon juice, increase heat to medium high and reduce until half of the liquid has evaporated, approximately 3 to 5 minutes.
4. Stir in the tomatoes, artichokes, cream, sugar, salt and pepper.
5. Turn off the heat. Add the butter one piece at a time while stirring to incorporate. Once all the butter has been added, stir in the basil.

6. Divide the goat cheese into 6 equal portions. During the last 2 minutes of cooking time for the chicken, top with the goat cheese.
7. Serve the cheese topped chicken immediately with the sauce spooned over top.
8. Garnish with the reserved lemon zest.

Makes 6 portions

SEAFOOD

Easiest Mussels Recipe Ever

Garlic Roasted Crab

Creole Halibut BBQ Pouches

Pastry Wrapped Wild Mushroom Halibut

Scampi

Spanish Paella

Steamed Mussels in Red Wine & Garlic

Tomato & Sausage Clams

Easiest Mussels Recipe Ever

"If you love mussels, what could be easier?"

1 – 430ml jar of store bought salsa
1 – 355ml can of beer
60 – 100 live mussels

1. Add the salsa and beer to a large pan and bring to a boil over high heat.
2. Add the live, cleaned, mussels to the pan. Cover and cook until the mussels have steamed open, approximately 2 minutes.
3. Discard any mussels that didn't open and then serve the mussels with the broth and big chunks of crusty bread... and a mug of beer (optional, of course).

Garlic Roasted Crab

"A great way to cook live crab – better than boiling them whole"

2 live crabs
1 head of garlic, chopped
1/2 cup butter
1/2 cup white wine
Juice of 1 - 2 lemons
Sprinkle of sugar, and salt & pepper

1. Preheat oven to 400 degrees.
2. Kill crabs by knocking them upside down on the head to stun them, holding all legs on one side with one hand, then rip the shell off (in the opposite direction of the hand holding the legs) – immediately chop the body in half. Clean the crab by removing the feathery gills, innards, apron, etc. Rinse with water and chop into leg segments.
3. Place crab pieces in one or two roasting pans. Add the garlic, butter, wine, lemon juice, sugar, and season with salt & pepper.
4. Seal the pans with tin foil and roast for 20 - 30 minutes.
5. Remove the foil and serve crab pieces hot with some of the broth.

Creole Halibut BBQ Pouches

"The trinity of bell pepper, celery & onion; along with garlic, tomatoes, thyme, sweet smoked paprika and cayenne, give this seafood dish delicious Creole flavour"

4 halibut filets, approx. 100g - 200g each
Salt & pepper
12 cherry tomatoes, quartered
1 stalk celery, sliced thin
1 small yellow bell pepper, cut into small short strips
4 garlic cloves, minced
8 thin slices onion
12 fresh thyme sprigs
2 tsp smoked sweet paprika
Ground cayenne pepper, optional
1 tsp sugar
4 tbsp cold butter
1 lemon

1. Preheat BBQ grill with high heat.
2. Cut 8 pieces of heavy duty aluminum foil – 12 inches x 18 inches. Lay 2 pieces of foil on top of each other to make 4 separate double-layer foil bases.
3. Place each filet, skin side down, in the center of one half of each of the foil bases, and season each filet liberally with salt and pepper.
4. Top each filet evenly with 3 quartered tomatoes, equal amounts of celery, equal amounts of bell pepper, 1 minced garlic clove, 2 thin slices of onion, 3 sprigs of thyme, 1/2 tsp paprika, pinch of cayenne, 1/4 tsp sugar, and season with more salt & pepper.
5. Top each mound with a 1 tbsp pat of butter.
6. Seal the pouches by folding over the foil in half longwise over the vegetable covered fish. Starting at one end, fold in and crimp the edges of the foil tightly and work around the whole open side of the foil to form a semi-circle pouch. It must be tightly sealed to keep all the steam and juices in the pouch.
7. Place the pouches on the hot BBQ grill and reduce heat to medium low. Close the lid and cook for approximately 12 to 15 minutes while

trying to maintain a cooking temperature of 375 degrees F on your BBQ's built-in gauge.

8. Remove pouches from the grill and let sit for 5 minutes before opening. The internal temperature of the fish should be 140-150 degrees F.

9. Cut open each pouch, squeeze over a bit of fresh lemon juice, and serve immediately.

Makes 4 portions

*Alternatively you can cook these pouches in the oven at 450 - 475 degrees F for 12 to 15 minutes.

Pastry Wrapped Wild Mushroom Halibut

"If fresh halibut filets are not available, use frozen – just thaw and pat them dry."

2 tbsp butter
1/2 medium onion, diced small
6 garlic cloves, minced
salt & pepper
1 pound mixed variety of mushrooms, sliced
    - preferably portabella, shitake, & oyster mushrooms
1/4 cup white wine
1/2 cup whipping cream
1 tsp sugar
2 pounds fresh, boneless halibut filets
2 – 397g pkgs of frozen puff pastry, thawed & chilled
All purpose flour
1 egg, mixed with 1 tbsp water
lots of fresh chives
1 lemon

1. Preheat oven to 400 degrees.
2. Over medium heat, melt butter in a large non-stick pan.
3. Add the onions, garlic, and season with salt & pepper. Cook until soft, approximately 2 – 3 minutes, stirring occasionally.
4. Add the sliced mushrooms and the white wine. Season with more salt & pepper. Turn the heat to medium-high and cook until soft, approximately 3 minutes, stirring occasionally.
5. Stir in the whipping cream and sugar. Taste & re-season if necessary, and remove from the heat.
6. Cut the fish into 6 equal portions and lightly season both sides with salt & pepper.
7. Cut pastry into 6 equal portions. On a lightly floured surface, roll out pastry portions into rectangles large enough to enclose each piece of fish.
8. Place each piece of fish on a portion of pastry, and top each one with 1/6 of the mushroom mixture, approximately 3 – 4 tablespoons. Add 2 sprigs of chives, chopped to each portion.

9. With a pastry brush, moisten all of the edges of the pastry with egg wash. Enclose each portion by folding up the sides and tucking underneath to completely enclose the halibut pieces.
10. Place pastry packets on a parchment paper lined baking sheet and bake for 25 minutes until golden brown.
11. Garnish each portion with a twist of lemon and chopped fresh chives.

Makes 6 portions

Scampi

"Great as an appetizer, main course, or a side dish to a seafood feast!"

1/2 cup extra virgin olive oil
1 head (10 – 12 cloves) garlic, minced
680g (1.5 pounds) large raw prawns, peeled & de-veined, tail-on
1 cup finely chopped fresh parsley
Juice of 1/2 lemon
Salt & pepper
Extra lemon wedges for serving

1. Place the oil and garlic in a large non-stick pan. Turn the heat to medium-low and heat to infuse the oil with garlic flavour, approximately 15 minutes. Be careful not to burn the garlic – you may need to lower the heat halfway through the 15 minutes.
2. Add the prawns and increase the heat to medium-high. Cook just until they have turned pink, tossing frequently – DO NOT OVER COOK.
3. Remove from the heat. Stir in the parsley and lemon juice. Season to taste with salt and pepper.
4. Serve immediately, spooning the oil "sauce" over the prawns.

Makes 4 to 6 portions as an appetizer

Spanish Paella

12 boneless skinless chicken thighs
Salt & pepper
1/4 cup olive oil
340g raw medium prawns, about 30 in total
1 medium white onion, diced small
1 – 398ml can crushed tomatoes
1 tbsp salt
1 tbsp sugar
2 tbsp sweet smoked paprika
6 cups chicken stock
2 bay leaves
2 cups short grain rice
1 cup frozen peas, thawed
1 medium red bell pepper, sliced into ¼ inch strips
3 garlic cloves, minced
2 precooked chorizo sausages (approx.250g), cut into half inch slices/chunks
20 thin asparagus spears, cut into 1 inch pieces

1. Preheat oven to 400 degrees. Season chicken thighs with salt and pepper – bake for 12 minutes and set aside.
2. While chicken is baking, heat a 14-inch paella pan over medium-high heat until hot. Add the oil and once the oil is hot add the prawns. Stirring constantly, cook the prawns until done, approximately 1 minute. Remove from pan with a slotted spoon and set aside.
3. Add the diced onion to the pan and cook until soft and lightly browned, stirring occasionally, approximately 2 to 3 minutes.
4. Stir in the tomatoes, salt, sugar, and paprika.
5. Stir in the chicken stock and bay leaves. Bring to a boil.
6. Add the rice and stir well to distribute evenly. Reduce the heat to medium-low, add the chicken thighs and simmer for 10 minutes.
7. Stir thoroughly to loosen any rice stuck to the bottom of the pan.
8. Stir in the peas, bell pepper, garlic, and sausage. Cook for 20 more minutes, stirring every five minutes to keep the rice from sticking to the bottom of the pan.

9. Taste and re-season if necessary.
10. Add the asparagus and the reserved prawns and cook for 2 more minutes.

Makes 8 to 10 portions

Steamed Mussels in Red Wine & Garlic

"Serve with big chunks of crusty bread to soak up the broth."

36 - 48 live mussels
1 tbsp olive oil
796ml can of diced tomatoes, drained
1 head of garlic, peeled and minced
2 tsp white sugar
Salt & fresh cracked pepper
1 cup red wine
1/4 cup fresh chopped parsley (plus more for garnish)
Lemon slices or wedges

1. Clean and de-beard the mussels.
2. Heat heavy bottomed large pan over medium-high heat. Add the olive oil, tomatoes, and garlic, and season with the sugar, salt & fresh cracked pepper. Sauté for about 1 – 2 minutes.
3. Add the red wine and bring to a boil.
4. Add the mussels and parsley; cover with a lid and steam until the mussels open.
5. Remove from the heat. Taste and re-season with salt and pepper, if necessary.
6. Serve in bowls accompanied with a crusty loaf of bread to soak up the broth. Garnish with lemon and extra fresh parsley.

Makes 4 portions as an appetizer, or 2 portions as a main course.

Tomato & Sausage Clams

"This is one of my favourites! My version of "surf & turf". Nothing beats sitting down with a big bowl of this with a glass of wine and a big chunk of crusty bread!"

300g mild Italian sausage
2 tbsp extra virgin olive oil
1 head (8-12 cloves) garlic, minced
1 tbsp fennel seed
2 tsp dried oregano
1 tsp dried thyme
1 – 796ml can diced tomatoes, drained
1/2 cup white wine
3 bay leaves
1 tsp sugar
1kg fresh live littleneck clams, scrubbed
Salt & pepper
Fresh parsley, chopped, for garnish
Fresh lemon wedges
Large crusty loaf of Italian bread

1. Squeeze sausage out of casings into a large heavy bottomed pan over medium to medium-high heat. Add the olive oil, garlic, fennel, oregano, and thyme. While pan is heating, mix together while breaking up the sausage with a wooden spoon. Cook for approximately 4 – 6 minutes, stirring occasionally, until sausage is cooked through.
2. Add the tomatoes, wine, bay leaves, and sugar.
3. Bring to a boil. Add the clams, cover, and cook until the clams have opened, approximately 4 – 5 minutes.
4. Discard the bay leaves and any unopened clams.
5. Season to taste with salt & pepper.
6. Serve in large bowls with plenty of the broth for bread dipping.
7. Garnish with sprinkles of freshly chopped parsley and lemon wedges, and serve with big chunks of crusty bread and a glass of chardonnay.

Makes 4 portions

RECIPE NOTES

SIDE DISHES

Black Bean Succotash

Colcannon

Garlic Mashed Potatoes

Dixie's Baked Beans

Maple Mashed Sweet Potatoes

Linguine in Roasted Corn Chipotle Cream Sauce

Roasted Greek Potatoes

Louisiana Red Beans & Rice

Scalloped Potatoes Gratin

Soft Polenta

Wild Mushroom Risotto

Black Bean Succotash

"Succotash is traditionally a side-dish made with steamed lima beans"

3 cups frozen corn kernels thawed and drained
1 - 540 ml can black beans rinsed and drained
1 small zucchini quartered and sliced thin
1 large red bell pepper diced small
1 jalapeno pepper diced small
2 garlic cloves crushed
1/2 cup cilantro coarsely chopped
3 tsp salt
Pinch of ground black pepper
2 tbsp olive oil

1. Combine all ingredients except oil in a bowl and mix thoroughly. (Jalapeno seeds and membrane can be eliminated for a milder dish.)
2. Heat heavy bottom pan over medium heat.
3. Add vegetable mixture to pan and cook until heated through, stirring occasionally.

Makes 8-12 servings as a side dish

Colcannon

"A classic Irish side dish made with basic staple ingredients. Best served with Guinness Cream Sauce."

4 extra-large russet potatoes, peeled and diced one-half inch
5 cups shredded (or thinly sliced) green cabbage
1 small onion, diced small
6 large cloves of garlic, minced
3/4 cup butter
4 tsp salt
1 tsp pepper
3/4 cup whipping cream
Fresh chopped parsley, for garnish

1. Steam the diced potatoes over boiling water until tender, approximately 20 minutes.
2. While the potatoes are steaming, melt 1/4 cup of the butter in a large pan over medium heat until it just starts foaming. Add the cabbage, onion, garlic and 1 tsp of the salt to the pan and cook until mostly soft, while stirring occasionally. Approximately 15 minutes.
3. Cube the remaining 1/2 cup butter and add it to the steamed potatoes along with the other 3 tsp salt and the 1 tsp pepper. Mash until thoroughly combined.
4. Stir the cabbage mixture and cream into the potatoes until thoroughly combined. Taste and re-season if necessary.
5. Serve immediately with Guinness Cream Sauce.

Make approximately 6 to 10 side portions

Garlic Mashed Potatoes

"These will spoil you for any other mashed potatoes – very rich and flavourful"

5 russet potatoes, peeled and diced approximated 1/2 inch
1/2 cup butter, cubed
6 – 8 garlic cloves, finely crushed or minced
2 tsp salt
1/2 tsp pepper
1/2 cup 35% M.F. whipping cream

1. Steam potatoes over boiling water for approximately 20 minutes until tender.
2. Drain water out of the pot, and put cooked potatoes in the pot.
3. Add the butter, garlic, salt, and pepper.
4. Mash by hand until almost smooth.
5. Add the cream and mash again until smooth.
6. Taste and re-season with salt & pepper if necessary.

Makes approximately 6 – 8 portions

Dixie's Baked Beans

"Big thank you to Aunty Dixie for letting us use her incredible baked beans recipe. These are probably the best baked beans you have ever had!"

450g bag dry small white beans, approximately 2 cups
8 cups water

1/2 pound (227g) bacon, chopped
3 – 284ml cans condensed tomato soup
2 cups water (not needed for slow-cooker method)
355ml can beer
1/2 cup ketchup
1 large onion, diced small
4 to 6 cloves garlic, minced
3/4 cup dark brown sugar
2 celery stalks, finely chopped
2 tsp dry mustard
3 tbsp molasses
1 tsp salt
Pepper to taste

OVEN METHOD
1. Pour the 8 cups water over the beans and let soak overnight – OR – put beans in a pot, add the water, bring to a full boil for 2 minutes, turn off the heat, cover and let sit for 2 hours.
2. Drain the beans and put them in a large oven proof pot. Add all the remaining ingredients and bring to a boil on the stove top. Cover and transfer to a preheated 350 degree Fahrenheit oven. Bake for 4 to 5 hours until beans are tender. Add more liquid if necessary during the cooking process if beans seem dry. Re-season with salt & pepper if necessary before serving.

SLOW-COOKER METHOD
1. Pour the 8 cups water over the beans and let soak overnight – OR – put beans in a pot, add the water, bring to a full boil for 2 minutes, turn off the heat, cover and let sit for 2 hours.

2. Drain the beans and put them in large pot. Add all the remaining ingredients (except for the 2 cups of water) and bring to a boil. Transfer to a slow-cooker/crockpot and cook on high for 6 hours, or on low for 8 to 10 hours. Re-season with salt & pepper if necessary before serving.

Maple Mashed Sweet Potatoes

1.5kg Sweet Potatoes (orange fleshed yams), peeled & cubed ½ inch
1/2 cup butter
2.5 tsp salt
1/4 tsp pepper
1/3 cup maple syrup
Chopped pecans or candied pecans for garnish, optional

1. Steam the sweet potato cubes for approximately 20 to 25 minutes until soft.
2. Mash the sweet potatoes with the butter, salt and pepper until smooth.
3. Mix in the maple syrup thoroughly, and serve immediately. Garnish with optional pecan pieces.

Makes approximately 6 cups

Linguine in Roasted Corn Chipotle Cream Sauce

"The roasted corn with the smokiness of the chipotles makes this a great side dish"

2.5 cups corn kernels
2 tbsp canola oil
Salt & pepper

2 tbsp canola oil
1 small onion, diced small
6 garlic cloves, minced
2 chipotle peppers (canned), minced
2 tsp salt
1/2 tsp fresh cracked pepper
1/2 small red bell pepper, diced small
1 tsp sugar
1.5 cups heavy cream
300g dry linguine, cooked al dente*
Salt & pepper to re-season, if necessary
Freshly chopped parsley, for garnish

1. Toss the corn kernels with the 2 tbsp olive oil and season with salt & pepper. Spread them on a baking sheet and roast in a 425 degree oven for approximately 15 to 25 minutes (depending on if fresh or frozen corn is used). Watch carefully to avoid burning and stir occasionally. They will be done when they are starting to caramelize (turn brown). Remove from the oven.
2. Heat a heavy bottomed, nonstick pan over medium heat. Add the other 2 tbsp of olive oil, the onion, garlic, chipotles, salt, and pepper and sauté until the onion and garlic are soft, 3 to 5 minutes.
3. Add the roasted corn, bell pepper, and sugar and continue to sauté for approximately 1 to 2 minutes more.
4. Stir in the cream and heat to a simmer. Remove from the heat and toss in the freshly cooked linguine. Taste and re-season if necessary.
5. Plate and garnish with fresh chopped parsley.

Makes 4 to 6 side dish portions

Roasted Greek Potatoes

"It is important to use a metal baking pan — it attracts more heat than glass casserole dishes. The darker the pan, the more heat it will attract to brown the potatoes properly!"

5 - 6 large Russet potatoes, peeled
1/2 cup fresh lemon juice
1 whole head of garlic, chopped
1 tbsp dried oregano
1/4 cup olive oil
salt & fresh cracked pepper to season
chopped lemon zest and fresh parsley for garnish, optional

1. Preheat the oven to 400 degrees.
2. Cut the potatoes into thirds or quarters, depending on how large they are.
3. Place all ingredients in a metal baking pan (make sure to choose a size where the ingredients just fit – not too big, or not too small) and mix to coat.
4. Bake until tender, approximately 1 hour, turning and coating every 15 minutes.
5. Lightly re-season with salt and pepper immediately after they are removed from the oven. Let cool 5 to 10 minutes before serving.

Serves 6 to 8 as a side dish

Louisiana Red Beans & Rice

"One of the staple dishes of New Orleans cooking, and is traditionally eaten on Mondays"

500g Italian sausage – hot or mild
2 celery stalks, diced small
1 medium onion, diced small
1 medium red bell pepper, diced small
6 garlic cloves, minced
1 tsp dried thyme
1 tsp dried oregano
1 tsp salt
1/2 tsp ground black pepper
2 cups long grain white rice
2 – 284ml cans condensed chicken broth
1.75 cups water
2 bay leaves
1 – 540ml can red kidney beans, rinsed and drained
Fresh thyme, for garnish

1. Squeeze sausages from casings into a large heavy bottomed pot. Discard empty casings.
2. Turn the heat to medium-high and break up sausage meat into small pieces with a wooden spoon while cooking until brown, approximately 10 minutes.
3. Turn the heat to medium and add the celery, onion, bell pepper, garlic, thyme, oregano, salt and pepper. Cook for approximately 2 to 3 minutes until the vegetables are soft but not brown, stirring occasionally.
4. Add the rice. Stir to coat with the fat and cook approximately 30 seconds until the rice becomes slightly opaque.
5. Add the chicken broth, water and bay leaves. Stir to combine. Turn the heat to high and bring to a boil.
6. Cover with a lid and reduce heat to low and simmer for 20 minutes.
7. Remove the pot from the heat and let stand covered for 5 minutes.

8. Remove and discard the bay leaves. Stir in the beans. Season with salt and pepper to taste, garnish with fresh thyme sprigs and serve immediately.

Makes 4 to 6 portions

Scalloped Potatoes Gratin

Recipe created by Katherine Desormeaux (Mrs. Chef Dez)
"These are my favorite scalloped potatoes"

4 large russet potatoes
1 large yellow onion
3 tbsp butter
1 cup grated old cheddar
1 cup milk
2 tbsp flour
2 cups whipping cream
1 clove garlic, finely minced
Salt & pepper

1. Preheat oven to 350 degrees Fahrenheit.
2. Thinly slice potatoes and onion on a mandolin.
3. Butter a casserole dish with 1 tbsp of the butter. Layer the potatoes, onion, and cheddar in 3 layers, seasoning each layer liberally with salt & pepper as you go, ending with cheddar on top.
4. Shake the milk and flour together in a well sealed container. Combine this mixture with the cream and the garlic. Pour over the potatoes and top with the remaining 2 tbsp butter broken into small chunks.
5. Bake for 60 to 75 minutes until potatoes are tender. Let stand for at least 10 minutes before serving.

Soft Polenta

"A classic staple of Italy. This recipe is so good I have even had old Italian women tell me it's the best polenta they have ever eaten! Serve on its own as a side dish, or as you would pasta with a tomato sauce."

4 cups water
1 tbsp salt
4 cups milk
1/2 cup butter
2 cups yellow cornmeal
100g Romano cheese, grated
2-3 garlic cloves, crushed

1. Bring water and salt to a boil in a heavy bottomed pot.
2. Add the milk and butter and heat over medium heat until butter is melted and mixture is almost at a boil again, stirring occasionally.
3. Add the cornmeal gradually while stirring constantly.
4. Continue stirring until mixture starts to become thick. Reduce heat to medium-low and stir constantly for 3 to 5 minutes, until it has reached desired consistency. It should be the same thickness as porridge.
5. Remove from the heat and stir in the Romano cheese and garlic thoroughly.
6. Serve immediately, alone or with your favorite pasta sauce.

Makes approximately 9 cups

Wild Mushroom Risotto

"Arborio rice is the classic rice used in risotto – it becomes very creamy as it is stirred and the liquids are absorbed. A delicious side dish – well worth the effort!"

5 cups chicken broth
4 tbsp olive oil
1 medium sized shallot, minced
3 garlic cloves, minced
1 pound mixed variety of mushrooms, sliced
1/2 tsp salt
2 cups Arborio rice
1 cup white wine
1/2 cup grated asiago cheese
salt & fresh cracked pepper to taste

1. Simmer the chicken broth in a small pot.
2. Heat a separate heavy bottomed pot over medium heat. Add 2 tbsp of the olive oil, and sauté the shallot and garlic briefly (about 1 minute) stirring frequently.
3. Add the mushrooms, the other 2 tbsp of oil, and the salt – cook, stirring occasionally, until the mushrooms reduce in volume slightly; about 2-3 minutes.
4. Add the dry rice and cook for about 3-4 minutes until rice starts to look opaque, stirring frequently.
5. Add the white wine and cook until all the liquid is almost gone, stirring constantly.
6. Start ladling warm chicken broth one ladle at a time until each one is almost absorbed, before adding the next ladle. Keep doing this until all the broth has been absorbed (about 15-20 minutes) stirring constantly.
7. Remove the pot from the heat, and stir in the grated cheese.
8. Season to taste with salt and fresh cracked pepper and serve immediately.

Makes 4 to 6 portions

DESSERTS

Blueberry Bread Pudding

Cranberry Bread Pudding

Picture Perfect Pie Pastry

Creamy Lime Custard Pie

Crème Caramel

Guinness Brownies

Lemon Soufflés

Pumpkin Chiffon Pie

Rum Flambéed Bananas

Sweet Biscuits

Blueberry Bread Pudding

1 – 454g (1 pound) French loaf
4 large eggs, beaten
1.25 cups sugar
1 tsp vanilla extract
1 tsp ground cinnamon
1/4 tsp salt
Zest from 2 lemons, finely chopped
2 cups 10%MF cream (half and half)
2 cups milk (2%MF or 3.5%Homogenized)
1.5 to 2 cups blueberries (fresh or thawed frozen)
Vanilla bean ice cream, optional

1. Preheat oven to 400 degrees. Tear the French bread into approximate 1 inch to 2 inch chunks and spread evenly on a large baking sheet. Bake in the oven for 10 minutes, tossing the pieces around about halfway through. Remove from the oven and let sit while you prepare the rest of the pudding.
2. Decrease the oven temperature to 350 degrees and prepare a 9x13-inch baking dish by buttering it.
3. In a large bowl, combine the eggs, sugar, vanilla, cinnamon, salt, and the zest thoroughly. Whisk in the cream and milk. Add the toasted bread pieces and toss together thoroughly with your hands. Let sit for 10 minutes for the bread pieces to absorb.
4. Put one half of the custard soaked bread mixture into the prepared baking dish and top with half of the blueberries. Add the remaining bread mixture (and scrape all liquid from the bowl) to the dish and top with the remaining blueberries. Bake for approximately 1 hour until the top browns and puffs up. Also an inserted butter knife should come out clean.
5. Let sit for at least 10 to 15 minutes before serving warm with vanilla bean ice cream.

Makes 10 to 12 portions

Cranberry Bread Pudding

1 – 454g (1 pound) French loaf
4 large eggs, beaten
1.25 cups sugar
1 tsp vanilla extract
1 tsp ground cinnamon
1/4 tsp salt
Zest from 2 lemons, finely chopped
2 cups 10%MF cream (half and half)
2 cups milk (2%MF or 3.5%Homogenized)
3/4 cup sweetened dried cranberries
3/4 cup cranberries (fresh or frozen), halved
Vanilla bean ice cream, optional

1. Preheat oven to 400 degrees. Tear the French bread into approximate 1 inch to 2 inch chunks and spread evenly on a large baking sheet. Bake in the oven for 10 minutes, tossing the pieces around about halfway through. Remove from the oven and let sit while you prepare the rest of the pudding.
2. Decrease the oven temperature to 350 degrees and prepare a 9x13-inch baking dish by buttering it.
3. In a large bowl, combine the eggs, sugar, vanilla, cinnamon, salt, and the zest thoroughly. Whisk in the cream and milk. Add the toasted bread pieces and the dried cranberries and toss together thoroughly with your hands. Let sit for 10 minutes for the bread pieces to absorb.
4. Put one half of the custard soaked bread mixture into the prepared baking dish and top with half of the fresh/frozen halved cranberries. Add the remaining bread mixture (and scrape all liquid from the bowl) to the dish and top with the remaining fresh/frozen halved cranberries. Bake for approximately 1 hour until the top browns and puffs up. Also an inserted butter knife should come out clean.
5. Let sit for at least 10 to 15 minutes before serving warm with vanilla bean ice cream.

Makes 10 to 12 portions

Picture Perfect Pie Pastry

Recipe created by Katherine Desormeaux (Mrs. Chef Dez)

"I like to cut in the shortening and grate the butter for the optimum texture and flavour. This is the combination I prefer, but you can feel free to play around with the ratio of butter to shortening as long as you use a total of 2 1/4 cups of fat. Shortening contributes to a lighter pastry and butter makes a more flavourful pastry."

5 cups flour
3 tsp brown sugar
1 tsp salt
1 tsp baking powder
1 pound shortening very cold
1/4 cup butter very cold
1 egg
1 tbsp white vinegar
Water

1. Combine flour, sugar, salt and baking powder.
2. Cut in shortening with a pastry cutter then, using a medium sized grater, grate the butter in and stir to distribute.
3. In a liquid measuring cup, lightly beat egg and vinegar and add enough water to fill to 3/4 cup measure. Stir into the flour mixture just until moistened, and divide the dough into four equal portions.
4. Shape each into a flat disk and wrap in plastic wrap. Refrigerate for at least 1/2 hour, and then roll out.

This recipe makes enough pastry for two double-crusted pies, and it freezes well.

Creamy Lime Custard Pie

Recipe created by Katherine Desormeaux (Mrs. Chef Dez)

"The optional food colouring enhances the presentation of the pie with a bright green lime appeal"

<u>Crust</u>
1/4 recipe of Picture Perfect Pie Pastry (previous page)

<u>Pie Filling</u>
1 cup sugar
6 tbsp cornstarch
1/4 tsp salt
2 cups milk
3 egg yolks, beaten
1/4 cup butter
1/2 cup cream cheese, softened in microwave
1/2 cup freshly squeezed lime juice
2 tsp finely chopped lime zest
2 - 3 drops green food colouring, optional

<u>Meringue Topping</u>
3 egg whites
pinch of cream of tartar
1/4 cup icing sugar

1. Roll out the pie crust and line a 9-inch pie plate. Trim the excess off the edge. Flute the edge for presentation. With a fork, poke holes in the bottom and sides of the crust to prevent air bubbles from forming. Blind bake the crust at 450 degrees for 12 to 15 minutes. Let cool at room temperature.
2. In a saucepan, combine the sugar, cornstarch, and salt. Slowly whisk in 1/4 cup of the milk. When smooth, whisk in the remainder of the milk. Turn the heat to medium-high and stir constantly until mixture is thick and bubbling. Remove from heat.
3. Slowly whisk 1 cup of the hot milk mixture into the beaten egg yolks, and then pour this yolk mixture back into the hot milk mixture in the

saucepan. Cook and whisk over medium heat for approximately 2 minutes until mixture is very thick and smooth.

4. Remove from the heat and stir in the butter. When the butter is melted, whisk in the softened cream cheese until there are no lumps. Stir in the lime juice, zest, and food colouring. Pour hot filling into baked pie crust.
5. Beat the egg whites and cream of tartar to soft peaks. Gradually add the icing sugar, beating until mixture forms medium/firm peaks. Immediately spread over the pie filling, ensuring to seal the meringue to the edges of the pie crust to prevent shrinkage.
6. Bake the pie at 350 degrees for 12 to 15 minutes or until meringue is golden brown.
7. Cool the pie to room temperature and refrigerate for at least 8 hours before serving.
8. Garnish with lime zest and twisted lime slices.

Crème Caramel
"My very favourite dessert — above all else"

2/3 cup sugar
1/3 cup water
1/4 tsp salt
2 cups whipping cream
1 cup milk
1 tsp vanilla extract or vanilla bean paste
1/2 tsp salt
One 2-inch strip of lemon zest
3 large eggs
3 large egg yolks
1/2 cup sugar

1. Preheat oven to 350 degrees Fahrenheit and grease 6 ramekins with butter.
2. Put the 2/3 cup sugar, 1/3 cup water and 1/4 tsp salt in a small heavy bottomed saucepan over medium/low heat until the sugar dissolves. When it starts to turn brown, swirl in the pan but do not stir until it turns dark rich brown, but not burnt. Immediately pour equal amounts into the prepared ramekins.
3. In another heavy bottomed saucepan, bring the whipping cream, milk, vanilla, salt and the lemon zest to just below a simmer over medium heat. Turn off the heat and let sit while preparing the eggs in the next step.
4. Whisk the 3 whole eggs with the 3 extra egg yolks and the 1/2 cup sugar until frothy.
5. Remove the zest from the cream mixture. Very slowly drizzle the hot cream mixture into the egg mixture while whisking constantly. Doing it slow will prevent the eggs from curdling.
6. Pour this prepared custard mixture into the caramel lined ramekins.
7. Place the filled ramekins into a large pan. Pour boiling water into the pan until the water level reaches approximately half-way up the outer sides of the ramekins.

8. Carefully put this pan into the oven and reduce the temperature to 325 degrees Fahrenheit. Bake for approximately 40 minutes or until the centers of the custards are almost set (cooked).
9. Refrigerate for a minimum of 2 hours and up to 2 days.
10. To Serve: Loosen the custard in each ramekin by running a butter knife all around the edge of the custard. Invert a plate over the ramekin. Quickly flip the ramekin/plate over and gently jiggle until the custard/caramel come loose. Remove the ramekin and serve on the plate.

Makes 6 portions

Guinness Brownies

"These are dark, rich, beautiful brownies with just a slight aftertaste of sweet bitterness from the Guinness. You will love these even if you don't like drinking Guinness."

Butter for the pan
1 – 440ml can Guinness, room temperature
4 large eggs
1 cup berry (superfine) sugar
3 cups pure semi-sweet chocolate chips (500g bag)
1/2 cup butter
1 cup flour
1 cup cocoa
Ice cream, whipped cream, or icing sugar for serving, optional

1. Preheat oven to 350 degrees. Butter a 9x13-inch pan.
2. Slowly pour the Guinness into a measuring cup or bowl to let the foam subside.
3. Beat the eggs and sugar together until light and fluffy.
4. In a double boiler, melt the chocolate chips with the butter, stirring until smooth. Remove from heat and add gradually while beating into the egg mixture.
5. Sift the flour and cocoa together.
6. To the chocolate/egg mixture, add the flour/cocoa mixture in three parts alternating with the Guinness in two parts, until well combined. The batter will seem very liquid.
7. Pour into the prepared pan and bake for approximately 30 minutes, or until an inserted toothpick in the centre comes out clean. Remove from the oven and let cool on a wire rack.
8. Cut into a maximum of 24 squares. Serve with ice cream, whip cream, or dust with icing sugar.

Lemon Soufflés

"If you love the flavour of lemon, you will love this dessert"

Butter for the dishes
2 tbsp butter
1.25 cups sugar
7 tbsp flour
1/2 tsp baking powder
1/4 tsp salt
4 large eggs, whites and yolks separated
2 tsp grated lemon zest
1/2 cup fresh lemon juice
1 cup milk

1. Preheat oven to 300 degrees. Butter a 5-6 small ramekins. Place them in a large pan that will allow them to be baked bain-marie style (surrounded by boiling water).
2. In a med-large mixing bowl, cream the 2 tbsp butter with the 3/4 cup of the sugar. Stir in the flour, baking powder, and salt.
3. In a separate bowl beat the egg whites to moist peaks, and then whip in the remaining 1/2 cup sugar until just mixed.
4. Beat the egg yolks. Add the egg yolks, zest, lemon juice, and milk to the dry ingredients. Fold in the whipped egg whites. Immediately pour into dishes.
5. Add boiling water to the bain-marie and bake for 55 to 60 minutes until golden brown and set. Let cool slightly on rack and then serve warm or room temperature.

Makes 5 to 6 portions

Pumpkin Chiffon Pie

Recipe created by Katherine Desormeaux (Mrs. Chef Dez)

"Beating the egg whites separately and folding them in makes for a light chiffon texture. A warm spicy twist on a classic family favorite"

3/4 cup dark brown sugar, lightly packed
1 3/4 cup (398ml) canned pumpkin puree
1/4 tsp salt
1/2 tsp ground cinnamon
1/4 tsp ground nutmeg
1/4 tsp ground ginger
1/4 tsp ground cloves
1.25 cups milk
2 eggs, separated
1 unbaked 9-inch pie crust

1. Lower oven rack to one level below center of oven. Preheat oven to 400 degrees.
2. Mix first seven ingredients together in a large bowl.
3. Stir in milk and beaten egg yolks.
4. Beat egg whites to soft peaks and fold into pumpkin mixture.
5. Pour into unbaked pie shell in a standard 9-inch pie plate.
6. Bake for 1 hour, rotating halfway through baking time.

Makes one 9-inch pie

Rum Flambéed Bananas

"A great dessert topping, but perfect with the Sweet Biscuits recipe in this chapter"

1/4 cup butter
1/4 cup dark brown sugar
pinch of salt
3 bananas, not overly ripe
2 – 3 tbsp rum

1. Add the butter, sugar, and salt to a pan over medium heat.
2. Cut the bananas in half lengthwise and then remove/discard the peels. Cut the banana halves crosswise into 3 pieces each. This will make 18 pieces.
3. Once the butter has melted, and the banana pieces and stir to coat. Once hot, carefully add the rum and carefully ignite with a long match or grill lighter. Shake the pan until the flames subside.
4. Cook the bananas until heated through and the sauce has thickened a bit, approximately 2–3 minutes.
5. Remove from heat.

Sweet Biscuits

2.25 cups flour
3 tbsp sugar
1.5 tbsp baking powder
1/2 tsp salt
6 tbsp frozen butter
3/4 cup sour cream
6 tbsp milk or water

1. Preheat the oven to 450 degrees, and spray a baking sheet with baking spray or line with parchment paper.
2. In a mixing bowl, combine the flour, sugar, baking powder, and salt.
3. With a coarse grater, grate the cold butter into the dry ingredients and gently toss together to mix/coat the butter pieces.
4. In a separate small bowl, stir the sour cream and milk together.
5. Pour the sour cream/milk mixture into the dry ingredients and gently start to mix together until both parts start coming together. Empty the contents onto the counter and work the dough gently until it almost fully comes together and is approximate shape of a 4x6-inch rectangle. **Be careful not to overwork the dough, as overworking will make a tough biscuit.**
6. With a sharp knife cut the dough into 6 biscuits, place them on the prepared baking sheet and bake for approximately 10-12 minutes until cooked and slightly golden.

Suggested Application
For each portion, cut 1 biscuit in half and place the bottom half on a plate. Top with vanilla ice cream, & rum flambéed bananas (recipe in this chapter). Then place on the top half of the biscuit, garnish with sauce from the bananas, a mint leaf, and serve immediately.

Makes 6 portions

RECIPE NOTES

MUFFINS, LOAVES, & BREADS

Banana Nut Muffins

Blueberry Bran Muffins

Cranberry Pistachio Banana Bread

Ham & Cheddar Scones

Irish Soda Bread

Peppered Cheese Bread

Spiced Apple Loaf

Yeasty Biscuits

Quick Cinnamon Rolls

The World's Best Cornbread

Banana Nut Muffins

Recipe created by Katherine Desormeaux (Mrs. Chef Dez)

2 cups whole wheat flour
1 cup brown sugar
1 tsp baking soda
1 tsp ground cinnamon
1/2 tsp ground nutmeg
1/2 tsp ground cloves
1 tsp salt
1/2 cup chopped nuts
2 eggs, beaten
2.5 (two and one half) cups mashed bananas
1/2 cup canola oil
1 tsp grated lemon zest
1 tsp vanilla extract

1. Preheat oven to 350 degrees and prepare an 18-cup muffin tin with baking spray.
2. Combine the flour, sugar, baking soda, cinnamon, nutmeg, cloves, and salt together in a bowl. Toss in the chopped nuts of your choice.
3. In a separate bowl combine the eggs, bananas, oil, lemon zest, and vanilla together.
4. Add the wet ingredients to the dry ingredients and mix until just combined. DO NOT OVERMIX.
5. Divide batter equally into the 18 muffins cups and bake for approximately 20 -25 minutes. Cool 5 minutes in the pan before removing to a wire rack to cool completely.

Makes 18 muffins

Blueberry Bran Muffins

Recipe created by Katherine Desormeaux (Mrs. Chef Dez)

"Tossing the blueberries in the mixture of dry ingredients will help keep them suspended in the batter instead of sinking to the bottom"

1 cup whole wheat flour
1 cup natural bran
1 tsp baking powder
1 tsp baking soda
1/2 tsp salt
1 cup blueberries
1 egg, beaten
1/3 cup canola oil
1/4 cup brown sugar
3 tbsp maple syrup
1 tsp vanilla extract
1 cup buttermilk or sour milk *see note below

1. Preheat oven to 375 degrees and prepare a 12-cup muffin tin with baking spray.
2. Combine the flour, bran, baking powder, baking soda, and salt together in a bowl. Toss in the blueberries.
3. In a separate bowl combine the egg, oil, sugar, syrup, vanilla, and buttermilk together.
4. Add the wet ingredients to the dry ingredients and mix until just combined. DO NOT OVERMIX.
5. Divide batter equally into the 12 muffins cups and bake for approximately 20 -25 minutes. Cool 5 minutes in the pan before removing to a wire rack to cool completely.

Makes 12 muffins

*Note: Sour milk can be easily made by putting one teaspoon of lemon juice or vinegar into a one cup measure. Fill cup with milk and let sit for two minutes.

Cranberry Pistachio Banana Bread

"The half slice of banana on the top of the loaf gives this loaf a unique recognizable presentation"

1/2 cup butter, room temperature
1 cup sugar
1/2 cup dark brown sugar
4 eggs
2 cups mashed very ripe bananas (approximately 4-6)
3 cups flour
4 tsp baking powder
1 tsp baking soda
1 tsp ground cinnamon
1/2 tsp salt
2 cups cranberries, roughly chopped, thawed if frozen
1.5 (one and one half) cups shelled salted pistachio nuts, left whole
1 yellow banana, sliced in half lengthwise

1. Preheat the oven to 350 degrees and prepare two standard bread loaf pans by spraying with baking spray.
2. Beat the butter and both sugars together with an electric mixer until thoroughly combined, approximately 2 minutes. Turn the speed to med-low and add 1 egg at a time until all 4 eggs are completely blended in. Stir in the mashed bananas.
3. In a large separate bowl add the flour, baking powder, baking soda, cinnamon, salt, and stir to combine. Add the cranberries and pistachios to this dry mixture to coat them with flour.
4. Add the wet egg/sugar/banana mixture to the dry ingredients and fold together until just combined – do not overmix.
5. Divide the batter between the two loaf pans and smooth out until even.
6. Place half of the yellow banana (cut side down) on the batter in each of the pans and bake for approximately 55 to 65 minutes, or until a toothpick inserted comes out clean.

Makes 2 loaves

Ham and Cheddar Scones

Recipe created by Katherine Desormeaux (Mrs. Chef Dez)

"Omit the ham to make cheese scones or omit both ham and cheese for plain scones."

2 cups all purpose flour
1/2 cup granulated sugar
1/2 tsp salt
1 tbsp baking powder
1/2 tsp baking soda
1/2 cup frozen butter
3/4 cup old cheddar, grated or cut into quarter inch cubes
3/4 cup ham cut into 1/4 inch cubes
3/4 cup buttermilk
2 tbsp whipping cream, optional

1. Preheat the oven to 375 degrees.
2. Prepare a jelly roll pan or two cookie sheets with baking spray.
3. Combine flour, sugar, salt, baking powder and baking soda in a large bowl. Using a medium fine grater, grate the butter into the flour mixture, stirring occasionally to coat the butter pieces in flour. Toss in the ham and cheddar cubes to coat with flour.
4. Add the butter milk and stir only enough to moisten. DO NOT OVER MIX.
5. Divide dough in half. Directly on the baking sheet, form each half of the dough into a 6-inch flat circle approximately 1-inch thick. Sprinkle the dough lightly with flour as necessary. Take the time to make neat smooth sides and surfaces.
6. Cut each disk into 6 wedges, but don't separate the wedges from each other – the support from the scones being side-by-side will help them rise better. Optional – brush the tops with the whipping cream for a shinier finish.
7. Bake for 15 to 20 minutes until golden brown.
8. Immediately upon removing from the oven recut the scones on the score lines. Cool for 5 minutes on the pan.

Makes 12 scones

Irish Soda Bread

2.75 (two and three quarters) cups all-purpose flour
1/4 cup wheat germ
3 tablespoons white sugar
1 tsp baking soda
1 tsp baking powder
1/2 tsp salt
1/4 cup butter, in small cubes
1.5 (one and one half) cups buttermilk

1. Preheat the oven to 375 degrees. Prepare a baking sheet with baking spray or parchment paper.
2. In a large bowl, combine the flour, wheat germ, sugar, baking soda, baking powder and salt.
3. Cut in the butter into this mixture until the butter pieces are approximately pea sized.
4. Add the buttermilk and stir until it just starts to come together.
5. Empty contents onto a lightly floured surface and gently press the dough together until it starts to become smooth and resembles a flattened ball approximately 1.5 (one and one half) inches thick. Do not over work the dough or it will become tough.
6. Gently transfer the dough round onto the prepared baking sheet. With a floured knife, cut an "x" across the top of the dough.
7. Bake for approximately 40 to 45 minutes until golden, and a toothpick inserted into the center of the loaf comes out dry.
8. Cool on a wire rack. Cut into wedges just prior to serving.

Makes 1 eight-inch round loaf

Peppered Cheese Bread

"A quick bread with tons of cheese and pepper flavours! For best results make sure you use old cheddar and fresh cracked black pepper."

2 cups flour (plus more for dusting)
2 tbsp sugar
4 tsp baking powder
1.5 (one and one half) tsp salt
1.5 (one and one half) tsp freshly cracked pepper
1 tbsp soft green Madagascar peppercorns, drained
2 cups grated old cheddar cheese
2 eggs, beaten
1 cup milk
1 tbsp melted butter
More pepper for sprinkling

1. Preheat oven to 350 degrees and prepare a 9-inch pie plate with baking spray and then dusting it with flour.
2. In a large bowl combine the flour, sugar, baking powder, salt, and pepper. Toss in the green peppercorns and 1.5 cups of the grated cheese to thoroughly coat with the flour mixture.
3. In a separate bowl mix together the eggs, milk, and melted butter.
4. Pour the wet mixture into the dry mixture. Stir until just combined and spread the mixture into the prepared pie plate.
5. Top with the remaining one half cup cheddar and more freshly cracked pepper.
6. Bake for approximately 30 to 35 minutes until the bread is solid and the cheese has browned slightly on top.
7. Let cool in the pie plate for at least 10 minutes before trying to remove it, and then let cool thoroughly on a cooling rack.

Makes one 9-inch round loaf

Spiced Apple Loaf

Recipe created by Katherine Desormeaux (Mrs. Chef Dez)

"Use 1 cup whole wheat flour and 1 cup all-purpose, or 2 cups all-purpose – but using 2 cups whole wheat flour will make the loaf too heavy"

1 cup whole wheat flour
1 cup all-purpose flour
1.5 tsp ground cinnamon
1 tsp baking powder
1/2 tsp baking soda
1/2 tsp salt
1/4 tsp ground nutmeg
1/4 tsp ground cloves
2 apples, peeled & diced 1/2 to 3/4 inch
1/2 cup butter, room temperature
1 cup sugar
2 eggs, beaten
2 tsp vanilla
1 cup buttermilk

1. Preheat the oven to 350 degrees and prepare a standard loaf pan with baking spray.
2. Combine the flour, cinnamon, baking powder, baking soda, salt, nutmeg, and cloves together in a bowl. Toss the diced apple into this dry mixture – this will help to keep the apple chunks suspended in the finished batter instead of sinking to the bottom.
3. Beat the butter and sugar together in a separate bowl. Add the eggs, vanilla and butter milk and mix thoroughly together.
4. Add the wet ingredients to the dry ingredients and mix until just combined. DO NOT OVERMIX. Place in the prepared loaf pan and bake for approximately 50 to 60 minutes, or until an inserted wooden skewer comes out clean.
5. Cool 5 minutes in the pan before removing to a wire rack to cool completely.

Makes 1 loaf

Yeasty Biscuits

Recipe created by Katherine Desormeaux (Mrs. Chef Dez)

2 tsp fast acting yeast
1/4 cup warm water
4 cups all-purpose flour
4 tsp baking powder
3 tbsp sugar
1 tsp salt
1/2 cup very cold or frozen butter
1.25 cups milk

1. Preheat oven to 400 degrees Fahrenheit.
2. In a two cup glass measure, dissolve yeast in the water and set aside.
3. In a separate bowl mix the flour, baking powder, sugar, and salt together. Grate in the cold butter with a medium sized grater and stir to distribute.
4. Add the milk to the yeast mixture. Add this wet mixture to the flour mixture. Stir and knead just until smooth. Shape the dough into a rectangle approximately 1.5cm to 2cm thick. Cut into 12 equal sized biscuits.
5. Prepare a baking sheet with baking spray or parchment paper. Arrange the biscuits on the baking sheet, cover with a clean towel and allow to rise for 20 minutes on top of the stove while pre-heating oven to 400 degrees.
6. Bake for 12 to 15 minutes.

Makes 12 biscuits

Quick Cinnamon Rolls

Recipe created by Katherine Desormeaux (Mrs. Chef Dez)
"Much quicker than traditional yeast raised cinnamon buns, and just as tasty!"

1 recipe of Yeasty Biscuits (previous page)
1/2 cup room temperature butter
1/2 cup firmly packed brown sugar
3 tsp ground cinnamon

1. Prepare the dough as mentioned in the Yeasty Biscuits recipe, but instead roll the dough into an approximate 25cm x 60cm rectangle.
2. Use 1 tbsp of the room temperature butter to liberally grease a 9x13 inch cake pan. Spread the remaining room temperature butter evenly over the rectangle of dough, leaving 2cm on the long edge without butter (to seal the roll). Spread the brown sugar evenly over the butter and sprinkle with the cinnamon.
3. Roll up the dough in a jelly roll fashion and cut into 12 equal pieces. Arrange in the prepared pan, cover with a clean towel and allow to rise for 20 minutes on top of the stove while pre-heating oven to 400 degrees.
4. Bake for 12 to 15 minutes.

Makes 12 cinnamon rolls

The World's Best Cornbread

"In my opinion, I am sure you have never tasted cornbread better than this!"

2 cups yellow cornmeal
1 cup all purpose flour
2 tsp baking powder
1/2 tsp baking soda
4 tbsp white sugar
2 cups grated cheddar cheese
2 cups frozen corn kernels
1 jalapeno pepper, diced small
1/2 red bell pepper, diced small
1 tsp salt
4 eggs, beaten
1 cup sour cream
1 cup milk
1/2 cup vegetable oil

1. Preheat the oven to 400 degrees and spray a 9x13-inch cake pan with baking spray.
2. Place the cornmeal, flour, baking powder, baking soda, sugar, cheese, corn, jalapeno, bell pepper, and salt in a large bowl – mix to combine.
3. Place the eggs, sour cream, milk, and oil in a second bowl – mix to combine.
4. Add the wet ingredients to the dry ingredients, and mix until just combined. Pour into the prepared pan and bake for approximately 30 minutes until golden brown and an inserted toothpick comes out clean.
5. Cut the cornbread into 12 to 24 equal portions.

Makes 12-24 servings

RECIPE NOTES

MISCELLANEOUS

Fresh Strawberry Margaritas

Health Nut Pancakes

Homemade Muesli

Lavender Lemonade

Oatmeal Breakfast Bars

Oven Dried Tomatoes

Popovers

Mushroom Omelet

Spicy Fennel Nuts

Fresh Strawberry Margaritas

"The trick to a perfect fresh strawberry margarita is to not puree the strawberries completely. By putting them in the blender <u>on top of the ice</u>, the ice will get crushed first before the strawberries."

1/3 to 1/2 cup tequila
1 tbsp orange brandy or regular brandy
2.5 tbsp sugar
1/4 tsp salt
3 cups large ice cubes
20 whole fresh strawberries, green tops removed

1. In a large blender add the tequila, brandy, sugar, and salt.
2. Add the ice cubes.
3. Add the strawberries and replace the lid on the blender.
4. Pulse on high speed just until the ice has been crushed enough to allow the strawberries to start reaching the blades at the bottom of the blender.
5. Blend on high speed briefly until the berries are chopped but not pureed smooth. You should be able to feel bits of strawberries when tasting.
6. Serve immediately.

Makes approximately 4 cups

Health Nut Pancakes

Recipe written by Katherine Desormeaux (Mrs. Chef Dez)

"Buttermilk has a thicker consistency, so if you choose to use skim milk instead you don't need as much"

1 cup whole wheat flour
1/4 cup wheat germ
1/4 cup ground almonds
2 tbsp sesame seeds
2 tbsp ground flax seed
2 tbsp sugar
1 tbsp baking powder
1/2 tsp salt
1 egg, beaten
2 cups buttermilk, or 1.5 cups skim milk
1 tbsp canola oil

1. Combine the flour, wheat germ, almonds, sesame seeds, flax, sugar, baking powder, and salt in a large mixing bowl.
2. In a separate smaller bowl, combine the egg, buttermilk, and canola oil together.
3. Preheat a non-stick pan or griddle over medium heat.
4. Pour the wet ingredients into the dry ingredients and mix until just combined – DO NOT OVERMIX.
5. With a large ladle, pour a portion of the batter onto the hot pan. Once bubbles form and start to pop on the surface of the pancakes, flip over to cook the other side until golden brown.

Makes approximately 8 to 10 four-inch pancakes.

Homemade Muesli

Recipe created by Katherine Desormeaux (Mrs. Chef Dez)

"Use this as a yogurt or dessert topping or try it in a yogurt and fruit parfait for dessert or brunch"

2 cups large flake oats
1 cup bran flakes cereal
1 cup slivered almonds
1 cup sweetened coconut
1/2 cup wheat germ
1/4 cup sesame seeds
3 tbsp ground flax seed
1 tsp cinnamon
1/2 tsp salt
1/4 cup Splenda granulated sweetener or liquid honey
1/2 cup canola oil

1. Preheat oven to 400 degrees.
2. Combine and mix all of the dry ingredients (including the Splenda, if that is the sweetener of your choice). If you are using honey whisk it together with the oil.
3. Drizzle the oil, or oil mixture, over the dry ingredients a little at a time stirring well between additions.
4. Spread the mixture onto a jellyroll pan or two cookie sheets. Bake stirring every 5 minutes until browned (approximately 15 minutes). Watch it closely to avoid burning.
5. Store in an airtight container.

Suggestions: Substitute sunflower seeds for the sesame seeds. Add raisins or your favourite dried fruit, after baking. Substitute your favourite kind of nuts for the almonds.

Makes 8 cups

Lavender Lemonade

Recipe created by Limbert Mountain Farm in Agassiz, BC, Canada
"This is our favorite lemonade and we make it for every picnic"

8 cups water
1 heaping tbsp lavender florets (flowers, fresh or dried)
Juice of 2 lemons, approximately 1/2 cup
1/2 cup sugar

1. Boil the water and remove from the heat. Add the lavender florets and steep at least 8 to 10 minutes (we actually make this the day before and leave the lavender florets in the water overnight to chill). Strain the florets out of the water and discard.
2. Transfer the water into a jar or pitcher. Add the lemon juice and sugar and mix thoroughly until the sugar has dissolved. Chill and serve each glass with a slice of lemon.

Makes approximately 8 cups

Oatmeal Breakfast Bars

"The benefit of oatmeal in a convenient bar. Great for Breakfast on the run too – Microwave each bar from frozen for 30 seconds on high power."

2.25 (two and a quarter) cups whole wheat flour
2.25 (two and a quarter) cups quick oats
3/4 cup raisins
3 tbsp ground flax seed
1.5 (one and one half) tsp baking soda
1.5 (one and one half) tsp cinnamon
1 tsp salt
3/4 cup butter, room temperature
1/2 cup Splenda Brown Sugar Blend
1 cup   unsweetened apple sauce
1.5 (one and one half) tsp vanilla extract
2 eggs

1. Preheat oven to 350 degrees and prepare a 9x13-inch cake pan with baking spray. Tip: Line the pan with parchment paper leaving the ends sticking out to make the uncut product easier to remove from the pan once cooled.
2. Combine the whole wheat flour, quick oats, raisins, ground flax seed, baking soda, ground cinnamon, and salt in a mixing bowl.
3. Beat the butter and Splenda Brown Sugar Blend together in a separate bowl.
4. Add the apple sauce, vanilla extract and eggs to the butter and Splenda/butter mixture. Continue beating until thoroughly combined.
5. Combine the mixtures in the two bowls together. It will be a very thick batter.
6. Press the mixture evenly into the prepared pan.
7. Bake for 18-20 minutes until firm.
8. Cool completely in the pan until room temperature before cutting.
9. Cut into 16 equal bars by removing the product from the pan first.

Makes 16 bars

Oven Dried Tomatoes

"If you can spare the time, the roasting of the tomatoes in the oven is well worth it — they become so intense in flavour! Make extra tomatoes and add them to pasta, sandwiches, salads, etc."

10 Roma tomatoes
2 tbsp olive oil
2 tbsp balsamic vinegar
1 tbsp dried basil leaves (not ground)
1 tbsp dried oregano leaves (not ground)
1/2 tsp salt
1/2 tsp fresh cracked pepper

1. Preheat oven to 200 degrees Fahrenheit.
2. Remove and discard any green tops of the tomatoes, slice in half from top to bottom (lengthwise), and place them in a mixing bowl.
3. Add the olive oil, balsamic vinegar, basil, oregano, salt, pepper, and toss to coat. Gently work a small amount of pulp out of tomato halves while working the flavours into the tomato cavities.
4. Arrange the tomatoes cut side up on a baking sheet lined with parchment paper.
5. Spoon the remaining liquid from the bowl over the tomatoes and lightly season each one again with salt and pepper.
6. Bake for approximately 5 to 6 hours, until the tomatoes have reduced by approximately two-thirds or three-quarters in size but are still moist. Remove from the oven and cool to room temperature.
7. Use in a number of recipes such as pastas, pizzas, bruscetta, grains, etc... anywhere you want incredible tomato flavor.

Makes 20 halves

Popovers

Recipe created by Katherine Desormeaux (Mrs. Chef Dez)

"These are a favourite with our family – either as a side with dinner, or for breakfast with butter and honey. For the flour use either all-purpose flour, or 50% all-purpose and 50% whole wheat – using all whole wheat flour will make them too heavy."

2 tbsp butter
4 eggs, beaten
1.5 (one and one half) cups milk
1.5 (one and one half) cups flour
1 tsp salt

1. Preheat oven to 375 degrees and grease the cups of a 12-cup muffin tin heavily with the 2 tbsp butter.
2. Whisk the eggs and milk together. Add the flour & salt and continue whisking until combined (some lumps are fine).
3. Divide the mixture evenly into the muffin cups and bake for 25 to 30 minutes until golden brown. DO NOT OPEN THE OVEN DURING THE BAKING PROCESS OR THE POPOVERS WILL DEFLATE.
4. After removing them from the oven, pierce each popover with a fork to allow the steam to escape.

*Variation: Try adding crushed garlic to the batter and sprinkling tops with parmesan cheese, or rosemary to the batter and cheddar cheese on top.

Makes 12 popovers

Mushroom Omelet

"It is important to use strong cheddar as it adds more flavour. An omelet has never looked or tasted this good before!"

4 or 5 large button mushrooms, thinly sliced
Olive oil
1 tbsp chopped onion
1 clove garlic chopped
2 eggs room temperature
1 tbsp water
Salt and Pepper
3/4 cup grated old cheddar, loosely packed
Chopped parsley

1. Reserve four slices of mushrooms.
2. Put the remainder of the mushrooms in a pan with 1 tbsp olive oil. Season with salt and pepper and cook over medium/high heat, stirring occasionally, until the liquid has evaporated and they have browned. Remove from heat and set aside.
3. In a separate small nonstick frying pan over medium heat add 1 tsp olive oil. When the pan is warm add the four slices of raw mushrooms (from step 1), onion and garlic. Season with salt and pepper and cook until soft; approximately 1 to 2 minutes, stirring occasionally.
4. In a small bowl, beat eggs with water. Add to the onion, garlic, mushrooms in the small pan.
5. When the eggs begin to set around the edges use a heat resistant silicone spatula to loosen edges. Turn the pan while lifting the omelet to allow uncooked egg mixture to seep under the cooked egg.
6. Once almost fully set, turn heat to low and season with salt and pepper.
7. Place 1/4 cup of the cheese on half of the open omelet. Put 3/4 of the sautéed mushrooms (from step 2) on top of the cheese and put another 1/4 cup of cheese on top of the mushrooms.
8. With the silicone spatula fold the uncovered half of the omelet over the mushroom cheese mixture.

9. Layer on top of the omelet with half of the remaining cheese and then all of the remaining mushrooms and then the balance of the cheese. Leave omelet in the pan over low heat until the cheese on top is almost melted.
10. Carefully slide the omelet with the spatula onto a plate. Garnish with chopped parsley and enjoy!

Makes one large omelet.

Spicy Fennel Nuts

"The anise aroma and flavour from the fennel seeds make these nuts a very inviting snack. If you don't have a mortal & pestle to grind the fennel seeds, a food processor or spice grinder can be used instead."

4 tsp fennel seeds
6 tbsp Splenda granulated sweetener
1.5 (one and one half) tsp salt
1 tsp cinnamon
1 tsp cayenne pepper
1 egg white
2 cups pecan halves
1 cup whole almonds

1. Preheat oven to 300 degrees.
2. Grind the fennel seeds in a mortal & pestle until mostly ground – they do not need to be completely ground into a fine powder.
3. Combine the ground fennel seeds with the Splenda, salt, cinnamon and cayenne in a small bowl and set aside.
4. Whip the egg white to moist peaks in a large bowl.
5. Fold the spice mixture into the whipped egg white until thoroughly combined.
6. Add the pecans and almonds and gently mix together until the nuts are thoroughly coated, and then spread evenly over a large baking sheet.
7. Bake for 25 minutes. Halfway through the baking time, use a metal flipper to separate the nuts from the pan and redistribute the nuts.
8. Cool the cooked nut mixture on the pan until they are room temperature – the nuts will crisp up as they cool on the pan. Serve immediately or store in an air-tight container.

Makes 3 cups

RECIPE NOTES

CHEF DEZ RECIPE NOTES

You will notice a number of recipes call for the ingredient 'sambal oelek'. It is a crushed chilli product that comes in liquid/paste form – usually found down the imported foods aisle at your local grocery store. It is a great ingredient to keep on hand and use in many recipes.

I have used the following two abbreviations in almost all of the recipes:
tbsp = tablespoon measure (15ml)
tsp = teaspoon measure (5ml)

ABOUT THE AUTHOR

Chef Dez (Gordon Desormeaux) resides in the Fraser Valley of British Columbia, Canada with his family. His passion for food and people is second to none and anyone who has attended his live performances would agree.

Thousands of have rekindled their romance for the culinary arts because of his infectious enthusiasm for bringing ingredients together.

www.chefdez.com

Author photo courtesy of Dale Klippenstein

Made in the USA
Middletown, DE
23 February 2019